Taming the Beast

Peter Tyrer was Professor of Community Psychiatry, now Emeritus Professor, at Imperial College, London, and is an expert in personality disorder. He was the founder president of the British and Irish Group for the Study of Personality Disorders and, from 2010 to 2017, Chair of the Work Group for Revision of the Classification of Personality Disorders (ICD-11) for the World Health Organization. He has published over 500 original papers and 31 books, including *Coping with Stress*, for Sheldon Press. In 2015 he was given the Lifetime Achievement Award by the Royal College of Psychiatrists in recognition of his research and clinical practice. He continues to be involved in research, mainly into nidotherapy, and is chair of NIDUS-UK, which supports the development of nidotherapy. All the royalties from this book will go towards the work of this charity.

Prof. Peter Tyrer   Foreword by **Stephen Fry**

TAMING THE BEAST WITHIN

Shredding the stereotypes of personality disorder

sheldon PRESS

First published in Great Britain in 2018

Sheldon Press
36 Causton Street
London SW1P 4ST
www.sheldonpress.co.uk

British Library Cataloguing-in-Publication Data
A catalogue record for this book is available from the British Library

ISBN 978-1-84709-475-9
eBook ISBN 978-1-84709-476-6

Typeset by Falcon Oast Graphic Art Ltd, www.falcon.uk.com
First printed in Great Britain by Ashford Colour Press
Subsequently digitally reprinted in Great Britain

eBook by Falcon Oast Graphic Art Ltd, www.falcon.uk.com

Produced on paper from sustainable forests

To Helen
for converting my personality weaknesses into strengths

Contents

Foreword

We are all, I hope, conscious of how much mental health has recently entered the national conversation. We are now more aware than ever of the prevalence of mental illness among the population. Issues of suicide, self-harm, declines into illness-induced drug and alcohol dependency, working days lost, friendships, families and educations blighted – these have all been ventilated in the press, online and in documentary, biographical and fictional representations everywhere. Schools, human resource departments and government agencies are more alive than ever to the need for destigmatization, understanding and help with the enormous burden that mental health places on the public purse and on public happiness and well-being.

It is an urgent crisis and, while the fire-fighting aspects of diagnosis and treatment remain supremely important, we cannot forget the need continually to parse, construe and comprehend the language and meaning of mental illness. In the USA the *Diagnostic and Statistical Manual of Mental Disorders* (DSM) has attempted to categorize the subject into a kind of taxonomy, much as we categorize plants and animals, dividing extreme and distressing mood swings, for example, into the diagnoses of cyclothymia or bipolar 1 and 2, and famously attributing to autism a 'spectrum'. The DSM stands as much as a kind of bible and manual for law courts, industrial tribunals and the insurance business as a genuine revelation about the meaning of illness. All well and good, but labelling reveals more about the state of society than the state of the human mind: a butterfly will flutter by just the same whether you call it a pretty creature, a Monarch or *Danaus plexippus*. Naming is important but can sometimes block rather than aid comprehension.

One division of mental health conditions that the general

population has picked up on is the apparent distinction between *mood* disorders and *personality* disorders. Those of us
who, like me, have suffered from the effects of bipolar disorder
like to congratulate ourselves on the purity and constancy at
least of our personalities. The illness, we say to ourselves, is like
the weather. It comes from outside of who we are. We might
be made alarmingly enthusiastic, exuberant, grandiose and
overconfident when in the grip of elevated moods, or grumpy,
silent, morose and pessimistic when depression descends on us
like a leaden cloud, but inside we are ourselves, all right and
tight. *Personality* disorders – that is, what the boogeyman suffers
from – they are dark and dangerous territory. To be told we suffer
from such threatens our sense of self and the very ownership of
who we are.

We know too much, alas, about how character, disposition
and behaviour can be apparently turned upside down by trauma
or infection to the brain to be confident that there really is
some stable enthroned entity called a personality, which, unlike
the liver or skin, for example, stands gloriously immune from
degradation and disintegration. But what is it? What marks
out a personality disorder? Is it what might have been called
a character flaw or moral degeneracy generations ago? The
term personality disorder (accompanied by such ascriptions as
'passive-aggressive' or 'narcissistic') can be hurled as an insult-
ing grenade at people whose ideas and behaviour threaten or
annoy us – look at how President Trump at the time of writing
is characterized. Are such distinctions and classifications useful
or meaningful? If so, how do they help us towards treatment?

So many questions are raised by this subject and yet the fear
raised by the greater stigma and apparently sinister aspects of
personality disorders has meant that they are much less readily
discussed and demystified than other forms of mental illness.
Now at last comes this exceedingly helpful and instructive book.
Professor Peter Tyrer has really let in the air and the light and

discusses the many aspects of personality with just the kind of clarity and authority that will be most useful to the general public and health professionals alike. The language he uses is clear and comprehensible; the ideas he raises will live with you for a long time.

Stephen Fry

Preface

Why have I written this book and who is it for? I have done so because I want to get the subject of personality disorder out into the open, untrammelled and unadorned, and also to correct a host of misconceptions about personality, including personality difficulty and disorder. These misconceptions are shared equally by the public and the medical profession, so I have a hard task in trying to change a great number of established views, most of them being highly negative.

There are many reasons for these misconceptions. The subject of personality disorder has been on the fringe of psychology and psychiatry for many years. Mental health has always been at the edge of medicine and is only just beginning to be understood fully and to achieve a measure of respectability. But if general medicine is like the Earth in the planetary system and mental illness winking close by as Mars, personality disorder is like the far off Pluto, only occasionally coming into view in its highly irregular wacky orbit and being the butt of jokes, many of them deriving from Disney and one of its well-known dogs. A suggestion made two years ago was 'Donald Trump, President of Pluto', and nobody thought anything could be more offbeat than that, unless it was 'Donald Trump, President of the United States'?

'Personality disorder' has also been rejected as a term by psychiatrists, and they are meant to know the subject. At various times it has been regarded as a form of moral degradation, a label for the tired, poor and tempest-tossed, a poor reason for not making a 'proper' diagnosis, and an expression of personal disgust. 'Personality disorder: The patients psychiatrists dislike' was the title of the paper published by two of my colleagues in 1988.[1] It is one of those papers in which the title conveys the whole content of the paper. It also reflects a remarkably accurate view across the range of the health professions. If we do not like the people we assess, and cannot stand the thought of treating them, it is tremendously useful to have a diagnosis that can be attributed and repeated as part of an allegedly careful clinical assessment. 'Mrs Smith may have anxiety/depression/phobias/ rituals but the presence of her associated personality disorder/ difficulties/issues/problems/handicaps/disability means that she is unlikely to be helped by our treatment, so I am sorry to say that your referral for treatment has to be rejected.' Personality disorder always fails quality control.

Even the experts in personality disorder have failed the subject. For the last 90 years they have been using a system of classification that has achieved the amazing combination of trivializing the subject to a set of cartoon images, yet also making it unbelievably complicated and riddled with jargon. So they have become a small group who understand themselves but not their other colleagues. As a consequence no one really knows where personality disorder begins or where it ends, and this only reinforces the views of those who can use personality disorder as a reason to reject people they dislike as untreatable. After all, if there is no body of knowledge that can challenge these primitive emotions they can continue to be used with impunity.

But things are changing. We are coming to the end of the tunnel of prejudice and gloom and have new ways of looking at personality and all its difficulties, as well as it strengths. A new classification of personality disorder will be published by the World Health Organization in 2018. This is the official world classification of illness (The International Classification of Diseases) and cannot be ignored. The proposed classification contains many of the ideas that have been put forward in this book, as I have been the chair of the working party that has been involved in the revision of the classification since 2010. The new system is a radical change and, because it is radical, it is likely to be resisted by many people, at least at first. This book, intended mainly for the general public, hopes to combat that resistance by allowing everyone to embrace the concept of personality difficulty and disorder, to recognize that most of us have some personality problems and, in so doing, appreciate to a much greater extent the problems of those who have more severe difficulties. Not least, I think it will help everybody in managing this very common condition.

So in this book I am tub-thumping the new system, explaining how it helps treatment and breaking a few barriers to understanding. It will take a generation to change old ideas but there is no reason why we should not start now. There is a new order to personality disorder, take it at the flood.

1

What is personality?

'Personality' is a strange word. Everyone seems to know what it is, but, when asked to define it, mumbles a few nonsensical platitudes, such as, 'the kind of person you are' or 'the way you get on with others'. It is both highly complex and yet deceptively simple. We seem to be able to identify personality features very easily, even in animals. We have two cats at home, one of whom is massively overconfident, strutting around house and garden like a country squire inspecting his estate, looks down his nose when visitors arrive as if questioning their right to be there, and the other, smaller and demure, who is quietly friendly but self-contained, curls up in odd corners, paper bags or large bowls and snoozes most of the day. The cats are twins and look rather similar, yet every visitor to the house immediately recognizes their different personalities from the way they behave.

Some definitions

So it appears we can look at people, and others, and come to conclusions about their personalities in a short space of time. For what it is worth, here are a few dictionary definitions:

- 'personality is the combination of characteristics and qualities that form an individual's distinctive character';
- 'the totality of an individual's behavioural and emotional tendencies';
- 'the quality or condition and being a person, the totality of qualities and traits, as of character or behaviour, that are peculiar to a specific person.'

I don't know about you, but I find these Greco-Latin definitions bland and meaningless, and eminently forgettable. We get a better understanding from literature. From the first time people started to write, there have been attempts to describe the fundamental essentials of what makes people as they are. It's a sticky subject, because so much of what we see is contrived for the consumption of others. So when the adolescent mixed-up Holden Caulfield in J. D. Salinger's *Catcher in the Rye*[1] calls almost everyone he meets a 'goddam phony', he is absolutely right. His fellow adolescents are all 'young folks puttin' on the style' (Lonnie Donegan's skiffle song in 1957). They are all trying to be what they are not, or at least not quite. And it's not just adolescents. We tend to act to suit the circumstances in all sorts of situations when we want to impress, but what others see of the person is not necessarily true. It sounds impressive to say 'I am what I am', as though you are laying your credentials on the line, but Holden would probably still regard all such people as phony. Although, if he was really impressed, he might call you a 'genuine phony'. It is only when you get older that you show your true self to most of the people around you, as by then you are too tired to act any more and no longer care what people think about you. It is then that the persona you present to the world is more closely aligned to what others say about you, and when these are completely in agreement you can probably say the world has a fair version of your personality.

Our famous wordsmith, William Shakespeare, got nearer to an accurate description of personality than most. 'Speak of me as I am. Nothing extenuate. Nor set down aught in malice,' says Othello before spoiling the rest of the speech by stabbing himself. In these three tiny sentences he recognizes that most of our own personality descriptions are faulty. They are distorted either by vanity or modesty and need additional back-up from others before they can be regarded as true (psychologists often substitute 'validated' for true, because they think 'truth' is too elusive). So if a valued and independent judge describes you honestly, and does not extenuate, this is getting close to the real nub. But then Shakespeare qualifies this as he also realizes all too well that personal opinions come into the description of others and there is a tendency to be tougher on criticism than praise. He said so himself: 'The evil that men do lives after them; the good is oft interrèd with their bones,' says Mark Antony of Julius Caesar, and here we are talking more about opinion than fact. We distort to fit our established views, and the dead cannot contradict us.

An example of personality spread over time

There is another aspect of personality that has been neglected in these descriptions – its fluctuations over time. There is a tendency to regard personality as a permanent quality like a fingerprint, a central marker that stays the same throughout the vicissitudes of life. We specialists in the field reinforce this by using words such as 'ingrained', 'persistent' and 'pervasive' to describe personality, but we are beginning to realize that we have got it wrong; exactly how wrong you will find out later. To illustrate this I would like to describe somebody I have known for many years. His name is Julian, and here I will try, like Shakespeare, to 'nothing extenuate, nor set down aught in malice', in describing him.

Aged 7

When Julian was seven, he was cheeky, mischievous and rather too confident. For some reason that adults were never able to decipher, he made people, mostly children, laugh a lot, sometimes uncontrollably. At school this behaviour at times escalated and children (mainly girls) were so convulsed they were removed from the classroom for being out of control and disruptive. Julian did not feel the slightest bit guilty about these obvious transgressions, regarding them as marks of achievement, and showed very little sympathy with those who had suffered as a consequence of his alleged humour. It even used to happen on the football field, where Julian discovered that it was easier to make opponents laugh and so lose control than it was to go past them in more conventional mode. His overconfidence was reckless in its scope. On one occasion a class teacher, fed up with Julian's frequent interruptions designed to tease and make others laugh, said, 'Since you're so clever, Julian, you might as well take over the class.' This turned out to be a serious mistake, because Julian did take over the class and prevented the teacher from resuming until an hour later.

Aged 17

Julian is now a much more studious boy, not known for his ability to make people laugh. He is looking ahead to university and has already decided that he wishes to help others and be in one of the caring professions. He works conscientiously and well in difficult surroundings. He is also able to concentrate well and does not mind doing his homework in the main sitting room of his house, as he can easily cut out all extraneous noise. This can go too far and sometimes he appears to be cut off from other people. His mother is perceptive but not too concerned and says to others, 'Julian is in a brown study', which sounds reassuring but not exactly clear. Julian is much less confident at school now. He hides in the background and does not have many friends. He has become absorbed in other things, joins a local natural history society and spends many hours helping out with a county survey of all the plants growing in Warwickshire (Shakespeare's county), in which the ambition of the organizers is to record every plant in each square kilometre of the whole county. He takes this very seriously, spending many days camping out in the area before recording and foraging during the day. He becomes highly competitive with other botanists counting plants in adjacent squares and challenges them, usually unfairly, when they find rarer species that he has not been able to find.

He seems to be happier with his plants than he is with people, as the plants are much more predictable. A lot has happened since he was seven.

Aged 27

Julian is now a medical practitioner working in a general hospital. He is married and busy with planning both a career and a family. He is more certain of himself again and is getting some of his old confidence back. He has transferred his interest in plants from the wild to the garden and is keen on helping the household budget by growing fruit and vegetables at home. Members of his family make fun of him for being very obsessional about weighing his produce regularly – tomatoes, potatoes, raspberries, carrots – and plotting the results on annual graphs.

He has a circle of friends, but is also a little competitive with them, and this can become a little irritating; he appears at times to be playing a game of one-upmanship with them. He is interested in sport, but now is more often a spectator than a performer.

Aged 37

Julian has moved up the medical ladder with its many rungs and is now working in the community as a consultant. He likes the independence of being a consultant. Within two years of his appointment, he made major changes in his work and moved most of his clinics into general practice, telling people these are much more pleasant environments than the Victorian hospital where he was originally based. Some of his more conservative colleagues think he is 'drumming up trade' by being more available to service-users, but he defends his position vigorously, some saying he does so with rather too much fervour. He is popular with other colleagues as he is reliable and will always help them out. The negative side of this is that he spends a little less time at home and both his wife and children say that he works too hard.

Aged 47

Julian remains a consultant and, although he enjoys his work, he feels he has done all he can do in his present post and is thinking of a move. He is keen on pushing the boundaries of practice and has attracted some attention as being a bit of a maverick. So, although he can always have something interesting to say and do, he is regarded as a little wild at times and breaks too many rules. So whenever there is the prospect of a new venture, either at home or at work, he can be sure to volunteer for it, often without thinking much about it beforehand. This sometimes involves taking risks. He argues that risk is endemic in his profession and if you never take risks you never make progress, but many others suggest he should be more cautious.

Aged 57

Julian is now in both teaching and clinical roles and has established himself as something of an expert, so is often in demand. Family life has suffered a little as his wife feels he is too wedded to his work, not enough to her, and now that the family is grown up, they should be spending more time together. Some of the original excessive self-confidence he had when he was seven has returned. He often speaks his mind without thinking of the sensitivities of his audience, interrupts people in the middle of conversation and has long diatribes against people who have annoyed him, politicians who express opposing views and petty officials who stand in his way. At times he can be plain rude.

Aged 67

Julian is now close to retirement, but still insists he has a lot to do and does not like talk of cutting down. He is advised by those who know him well that he ought to be less preoccupied with work and should not be so puritanical about enjoying himself. He gets more irritable with others who stand in his way and sometimes gets quite angry. This surprises many as he has not shown much anger before. He is beginning to slow down, but pretends he is just as fit and well as he was 20 years ago.

These are just snapshots taken over 60 years, but if accurate, show quite a few changes in personality at different phases in life. But are they accurate? I would very much like to think so, as Julian is me (Julian is my second name). I have tried to be as fair as possible and give a representative picture of my personality, but I am sure others would wish to add and amend, if not contradict, what I have written.

This is also a very limited description of my main personality characteristics at different times of life. I am not writing a biography; if I was, it would include (I hope) a more rounded picture of me, including more positive qualities, my likes and dislikes, attitudes, sense of humour, outside interests and a lot more about my innermost feelings. So, in one sense, all personality assessments are primitive and incomplete.

What I am really wanting to get over in this set of descriptions is that there are very important changes in personality over the course of life so, although parts of it persist, many parts change. It continually develops. This is particularly true in the early years. The contrast between a bubbly, gregarious 7-year-old and the studious, rather boring schoolboy of 17 is enormous, and, although there is more continuity later in life, you can see that irritability and intolerance are creeping in gradually as I get older. If you look at individual personality features you can see changes too.

Obsessional characteristics, such as devotion to work, taking on more responsibilities and getting more rigid and less tolerant of others who do not think in the same way, seem to gradually increase over the years. But, at the same time, irritability and anger also seem to increase, and these are very different characteristics. Risk-taking is almost at the opposite pole of obsessionality and yet this too seems to be present at the same time at different ages. So the idea that you can earmark someone's personality at the age of 18 and give it a clear label of persistence is patent nonsense. Everyone's personality, not just mine, is a mix of different features/traits/characteristics/elements, whatever you like to call them, that fluctuate over time, sometimes dramatically, especially in response to life circumstances. So we have to be very careful how we describe and order personality, and always be aware that the best we can do is to provide a rough template of what it really is.

Other views about personality

I have tried to be as accurate as possible in this account, but have omitted an important element. I am an identical twin and my brother (Stephen) therefore has exactly the same genes as me. So are our personalities the same also? No, they are not, even though there are many similarities. I am not going to embarrass him by describing his personality, because it would complicate matters and in some ways I would be wrong, but the simple fact is that, although we look and behave in very similar ways, we are very different in the ways we relate to others.

One of the sad features of those who study personality and its disorders is that too little attention is paid to personality strengths and resilience, as these can be very important in overcoming any (often more frequently perceived) weaknesses. So, I hope you would agree, what shows through the descriptions of my personality is that I have energy and drive, and do not give up easily. These are less demarcated personality features than weaknesses, but in many ways they are more important, because they are positive features that help me in adversity. Having drive and determination helps me enormously, but is not a universal plus. We also need to be aware that they may have negative consequences.

Many great historical figures had drive and determination

that helped to make them famous, but, nonetheless, managed to create havoc in other people's lives. Winston Churchill, Napoleon Bonaparte, Leo Tolstoy, J. M. W. Turner (the famous painter), Lloyd George, Adolf Hitler, Joseph Stalin, Stonewall Jackson – the list could become very long. But, you may well ask, what havoc did they create? You just need to look carefully at the lives of their families and close friends to understand that fame and importance come at a price for others. In identifying exactly how these people create trouble for others, the words 'single-minded' and 'egocentric' loom large, but I could be harsher and call it selfish. These people use their drive and determination to further a variety of goals, but in many cases it is very difficult to separate the person from the vision. In promoting a cause, they are promoting themselves. I certainly feel that there is a bit of this in me.

One of the features that is prominent in the account of my life is a tendency to act on impulse. I interrupt people, I forge ahead on schemes without always thinking them through carefully and I say things that I often regret later. This again can have positive qualities. I often take comfort in Shakespeare's metaphor, 'There is a tide in the affairs of men. Which, taken at the flood, leads on to fortune.' So there are many occasions in my life when acting apparently on impulse has been remarkably successful. This has included leading an expedition to central Africa when I was an undergraduate, applying for jobs without thinking what they entailed and speaking my mind when all around seemed to be hiding theirs.

In looking at the changes in personality over time, it is also easy to see the advantages of these at different times of life. When you are younger, you are fighting for a place in the world and often adopt different ways of behaving – we can call them roles – because we are not quite sure which is the best. We have less confidence in ourselves (except sometimes when we are very young) and can be buffeted by circumstances very easily.

So it is understandable why aggression is stronger when you are younger, why anxiousness and concern are stronger when you have a young family to protect and why obsessional features become stronger when you are less able to defend yourself.

A summary of personality

In taking all these points together, we can make the following statements about personality.

1 It is an essential part of functioning and behaviour and tends to be formed early in life.
2 There are some personality characteristics, more commonly called 'traits' (the second 't' is hard), that probably do persist throughout life. In my case, these are (a) a degree of egocentricity, (b) a tendency to act on impulse and (c) an obsessional attitude to work and other tasks.
3 All these can have positive and negative aspects.
4 Personality problems are shown primarily in relationships with others.

This last point is very important indeed. In every other form of mental illness, people can have their problems assessed in isolation from others. This does not mean that they do not have an impact on other people, but their fundamental characteristics can be examined by psychological, and increasingly by neurobiological, investigations. Personality is different. To assess it properly you have to look at interaction with others.

How others see us

Ah, others. This is where the nooks and crannies of personality difficulties can be exposed. Unless we are feeling depressed and miserable, we tend to give a better account of our personalities than others do. Generally, we like to feel good about ourselves and so suppress a large chunk of the negatives that we either never hear or choose not to hear when we do hear them.

So, although the celebrated Scottish poet Robbie Burns wanted us to have greater insight into others' opinions when he composed these magical lines,

> O wad some Pow'r the giftie gie us
> To see oursels as ithers see us,

He could have followed it with:

> But if the Pow'r could make this be
> Our lives wad be cloak'd in misery.

At various times in my life I have heard the words 'inconsiderate', 'rude', 'tactless', 'impossible', 'arrogant', 'boorish' and 'insensitive' applied to my behaviour or my personality. When I hear these words, I try to justify myself by explaining what I did in that specific situation or apologize for appearing what I was really not, but it is no use. These words keep coming up and I have to accept that they describe deficiencies in my personality or, at best, features that I would prefer not to acknowledge. What they are really describing is a negative impact of my behaviour on the feelings of other people and, when this becomes widespread, we have to think of personal difficulty and disorder.

As an exercise, my readers could go through exactly the same biography of personality that I have described for myself. When I started this chapter, I thought it would be relatively easy and pain free to describe my personality, but as I have gone on, and especially when describing some of my more negative features, I have felt increasingly uncomfortable. How can I really have been as difficult as that? Could I have offended so many people? Why on earth could I have not been more considerate? I suspect that all of us, if we are really prepared to be honest with ourselves, will find difficult questions to answer like the ones above.

So there we have it. Personality is straightforward but complex, sometimes fixed but more often changing, often hidden from ourselves but exposed to others, maddening and fascinating, tangible but elusive, but never really boring. We cannot escape what we are, but by understanding better, we can enhance our lives. 'Be yourself,' Oscar Wilde wrote, 'everyone else is taken.' Being comfortable in yourself is the goal of personality adjustment, and it is achievable.

2

Normal and abnormal personality

I hate writing these words. They suggest that all of us can be divided into two groups – those who have a normal, well-adjusted and harmonious personality, and another group, much smaller, which is impossible to like, difficult and antagonistic, and generally to be avoided at all times. But this is indeed how we describe personality – quite wrongly – in current mental health classifications.

One of the messages that I hope you will take away after reading this book is that this split into 'normal' and 'abnormal' is quite wrong, unhelpful and, I might add, potentially dangerous. We are all on a spectrum – some of us with minor, and probably insignificant, personality problems, while others have greater difficulties but are still not all that far away from the rest of us. So why do we make a distinction between so-called 'normal personality' and another group that is labelled 'personality disorder'?

Personality disorder and disease

The answer lies in the medical concept of 'disease'. Although most mental conditions are described as 'disorders', they follow the same set of constructs as 'diseases' in medical practice. People with a medical disease have a set of identifying characteristics that separate them from others who do not have the disease. So people with cardiac failure tend to be short of breath, have swollen ankles and legs, are unable to exert themselves without distress and have a range of abnormal signs on examination, such as raised venous pressure. The comparison with someone who has a healthy heart could not be more striking.

This distinction is important in practice. A person with heart failure requires a range of drug treatments to make the heart stronger and more efficient. The best-known of these is digoxin. The discovery of digoxin is an interesting and instructive story. A Scottish doctor, William Withering, was interested in medicine and botany and was always looking for new ways to treat disease. He was practising in the eighteenth century, when there were no treatments available for cardiac failure. In 1775, one of his patients came to him and was clearly in cardiac failure. 'It's no good,' he told the person, 'you have a bad heart and I cannot really help you.' He expected the man to die within the next few weeks, but the man was not giving up and went to see a local gypsy, who prescribed a secret herbal remedy. He recovered dramatically and was no longer in cardiac failure when Dr Withering saw him again.

Dr Withering was excited and determined to find out what was in the secret remedy, as he thought it might have been the necessary clue for an effective treatment. He searched for the gypsy throughout the byways of the Midlands countryside where he worked. Eventually he found her and demanded to know what was in the secret remedy. He managed to persuade her (possibly a bit of bribery was involved here) to let him know what was in her concoction. Dr Withering worked out from his knowledge of botany that the most likely active ingredient was the common foxglove (*Digitalis purpurea*) and found that the juice extracted from the crushed leaves of this plant (the drug, digoxin) was indeed a powerful and effective drug that improved the efficiency of the heart.

So, here we have a classic example of the value of the 'disease' concept. People in cardiac failure have a set of symptoms and signs (these are observations made by the examining doctor) that are consistent and indicate the cause of the problem. This leads directly to the selection of a treatment that will help that person, but would be of no value, and possibly even harmful, to someone who does not have that disease. So the simple split between cardiac failure and no cardiac failure is a very valuable one in practice.

But when we switch to abnormal personality, we find this notion ridiculous. First, it is very difficult to find common features that are only present in people with so-called personality disorder and absent in those who do not have the condition. Even more fanciful is the notion that a specific treatment might be plucked from a range of options to correct the abnormalities found in those with personality disorder. Yet we flatter ourselves into believing that we can make a distinction between normal and pathological personality that has the crispness and value of the identification of cardiac disease. Some go so far as to suggest a specific treatment for the condition.

Of course, psychiatrists do not really believe that they can diagnose personality disorder in the same way that physicians can diagnose cardiac failure, but unfortunately it is the only game in town. Others may play in superior stadiums with perfect turf, but in the sixth division the personality disorder players compete on a sloping pitch with molehills everywhere and keep falling flat on their backs when trying to score impressive goals. However, it is not just personality disorders that are in this position. Psychiatric disorders are regarded internationally as the same as medical diseases, but consistently fail the test of an independent measure (like heart failure) that allows a confident diagnosis to be made.

So why bother to make a diagnosis of personality disorder? Society demands a distinction and expects psychiatrists to be experts. People with abnormal personalities should not, it is commonly believed, be allowed to be in positions of responsibility, have the capacity to make major decisions, be in charge of vulnerable people, act as educationists and instructors or be involved in dozens of other activities where their judgement may be faulty or impaired. Again, this is ridiculous. It says more about the prejudice created by the term 'personality disorder' than any intrinsic differences separating people.

Formal classifications of personality disorder

Those with an abnormal personality are included in formal classifications under a general umbrella label of 'personality disorder'. The two classifications are given in the *International Classification of Diseases* (ICD), published by the World Health Organization (WHO), and the *Diagnostic and Statistical Manual of Mental Disorders* (DSM), published by the American Psychiatric Association (APA). The classification of personality disorder in the DSM has undergone what might be described as an unfortunate perturbation in its latest revision as it was not accepted for inclusion. It is currently being reviewed and refined so only the terminology used in the ICD's tenth revision – known as ICD-10 – is included here.

International Classification of Diseases (10th revision, 1992)[1]

These types of condition comprise deeply ingrained and enduring behaviour patterns, manifesting themselves as inflexible responses to a broad range of personal and social situations. They represent either extreme or significant deviations from the way the average individual in a given culture perceives, thinks, feels and, particularly, relates to others. Such behaviour patterns tend to be stable and to encompass multiple domains of behaviour and psychological functioning. They are frequently, but not always, associated with various degrees of subjective distress and problems in social functioning and performance.

Personality disorder tends to appear in late childhood or adolescence and continues to be manifest into adulthood. It is therefore unlikely that the diagnosis of personality disorder will be appropriate before the age of 16 or 17 years.

In the classification given in ICD-11, to be published in 2018, the above will be updated to include more detail. The final version has yet to be decided, but the main additions include mention of both self-functioning and interpersonal functioning, and maladaptive patterns of thinking (cognition) and emotions, expressed in terms of both the experience and expression of emotion and consequent behaviour. There is also likely to be a continuous time period of disorder of at least two years specified before which the diagnosis cannot be made, but no age limits (upper or lower) given (unlike in ICD-10).

These definitions are for professionals to use, however, not the general public. It is possible to summarize the essentials of personality disorder more simply, in one sentence even. This is mine:

> Personality disorder is a recurring condition that, when present, hinders mutual understanding in relationships, souring and damaging them.

This said, as will clearly be shown in the rest of this book, a single statement such as this is inadequate on its own; it is just the very start of a general guide.

However we interpret these words, it is not a very pleasant set of descriptions. I think the best way of summarizing the people described here are the three words my grandmother used frequently – 'not very nice', always said with a sniff and an upturning of the nose. Nobody likes being fitted into these different groups; what is more, when the words 'enduring', 'ingrained' and 'persistent' recur frequently, it seems to be clear that this not-very-nice state is not going to get better in a hurry. So these definitions and descriptions comprise a lexicon of misfits who seem to be beyond redemption as we all know, or think we know, that personality disorder does not change. This is one myth that will be busted before the end of this book.

Although the descriptions above might appear to be the end of the diagnosis, they are barely the beginning. Each diagnostic system has a set of categories of personality that are used more frequently than the general term 'personality disorder'. Where do these all come from and what is the justification for their use?

It is quite a long story. A German psychiatrist called Kurt Schneider, with a good eye for clinical detail, suggested, in 1923, a classification of ten personality types.[2] These were all called types of 'psychopathic personality' ('psychopathic' at that time was a general description of abnormal mental states – its modern equivalents we will come to later). These do not translate very well into English and the modern equivalents and their general meanings are shown in brackets after each one:

1 abnormal mood and activity (cyclothymic or up-and-down personalities)
2 insecure sensitive (paranoid and suspicious)
3 insecure anankastic (obsessional, abnormally fussy)
4 fanatical (driven, single-minded)
5 self-assertive (egocentric, self-important)
6 emotionally unstable (borderline)
7 explosive (impulsive)
8 callous (antisocial)
9 weak-willed (easily led and controlled, including dependent)
10 asthenic (inadequate).

This was not a bad classification for a subject that nobody had taken much interest in before, but it was based entirely on Schneider's own observations and, nowadays, would be regarded as a very low level of evidence to make a diagnosis. Essentially, these were opinions only.

Because there was nothing else to go on in the field, however, these terms took off. Both the *International Classification of Diseases* and the *Diagnostic and Statistical Manual* in the USA have maintained the general meaning of these terms and just fiddled about with the names. So, if we take the latest classification we have the following:

1 abnormal mood and activity (this has retained the term cyclothymic, but is now regarded as part of the bipolar spectrum (that is, it is a disorder of mood))

2 insecure sensitive (this is renamed 'paranoid')

3 insecure anankastic (this is retained as anankastic in ICD, but called obsessive-compulsive in DSM)

4 fanatical (this is the only one of Schneider's types to be lost)

5 self-assertive (this has become narcissistic in DSM, but there is no equivalent in ICD)

6 emotionally unstable (this has become 'borderline' in DSM, but is retained as emotionally unstable, subcategory 'borderline', in ICD)

7 explosive (emotionally unstable, subcategory impulsive in ICD, not in DSM)

8 callous (antisocial in DSM, dissocial in ICD)

9 weak-willed (dependent in both ICD and DSM)

10 asthenic (not properly represented in ICD or DSM).

What has been the reason for this longevity, nearly 100 years after they were first described?

To examine this, it is worth looking at one of the diagnoses in detail – narcissistic personality disorder.

It is fair to add that this is one of the most contentious of all the diagnoses and it has never been part of the international system of classification, but it does illustrate all the problems involved in trying to define a disorder in the personality grouping. It is also highly topical at present as 'narcissistic' is one of the adjectives most frequently applied to authoritarian world leaders, of which Donald Trump may perhaps be an example. If you have him in mind when reading the next few sentences you will get the full flavour. To help I will add a Trump tweet after each example.

Narcissus is the original model for this disorder. He was the Greek god who was so handsome – or, to be more accurate, thought he was so handsome – that when he saw his reflection in a pool, he could not take his eyes away from his beauty, was fixed to the spot and became a narcissus or daffodil as a permanent record of self-love.

It is not surprising, then, that in all the many definitions of narcissism, we find the same features recurring in different forms. These include self-importance (DT: 'wasn't I a great candidate?'), an overweening desire for admiration (DT: 'we should have a contest as to which of the networks is the most dishonest, corrupt and/or distorted in its political coverage of your favorite President (me)'), excessive self-importance and envy (DT: 'sorry losers and haters, but my I.Q. is one of the highest – and you all know it! Please don't feel so stupid or insecure, it's not your fault'), lack of empathy (DT: 'Can't believe these totally phoney stories, 100% made up by women (many already proven false) and pushed big time by press'), and a strong sense of entitlement ('all of the women on The Apprentice flirted with me – consciously or unconsciously. That's to be expected').

So it is not difficult to tune in to these different accounts of narcissism, but do these characteristics, if prominent, make for a diagnosis of personality disorder? Allen Frances does not think so. He was the chair of the Task Force for the fourth revision of the American DSM classification (DSM-IV) as well as being a personality disorder expert, and he was primarily involved in creating the criteria for the diagnosis of narcissistic personality disorder. He summarizes Donald Trump in these words: 'He may be a world-class narcissist, but this doesn't make him mentally ill, because he does not suffer from the distress and impairment required to diagnose mental disorder.'

It is when we turn to the interpretation of the features of narcissism that we realize how common they are. How many people in this celebrity-fixated world have fantasies of amazing success in their lives, particularly when they are young, and don't most people want to be admired? How do we decide what is excessive?

When it comes to envy, how many people do you know who are envious of others and/or feel that someone is also envious of them? I suspect it is a pretty large number.

We also need to remember that these characteristics are meant to be present over a long time period, perhaps indefinitely, as well as creating personal distress. How do we assess this?

All in all, we have to conclude that this is hardly a comprehensive assessment of a personality characteristic – it is more like a cartoon image exaggerating features we do not particularly like. These 'operational criteria', as they are officially called, may have some value when identifying the main features of an illness such as bipolar disorder, but they fall down badly with personality disorder and do not impress.

I was once at a meeting of the American Psychiatric Association where one of the speakers presented a light-hearted paper about research carried out on his university colleagues, which showed that between 70 and 80 per cent had narcissistic personality disorder. He described their single-minded obsession with their research, how important it was and how much they should be appreciated, yet how much of their work was resented by others (who were envious of its obvious success). They also felt entitled to a much higher position and status within their departments and the university than they currently held.

I reported this in an editorial in the *British Journal of Psychiatry* in 2008 and within a week of publication I received a letter from Leon Eisenberg, former Professor of Psychiatry at the University of Harvard in the United States:

Dear Peter

Your editorial is not only charming, it's profound, but it did contain one disappointing piece of news. You report that some speaker at a recent APA meeting 'identified 70–80% of clinical psychiatric academics in the US as satisfying the criteria for narcissistic personality disorder'.

  I thought my own massive study of the Harvard Faculty, which found even higher rates, would be published first, and now I discover that I have been anticipated, but thanks for writing your piece. It's fun, and it's thoughtful.

Sincerely

Leon

I think this simple message is a useful summary of the status of this category of personality disorder. Do we really need to consider it more?

I cannot leave the categories of personality without mentioning psychopathy. This is the court jester in the personality play; it fools and annoys in equal measure. It is not mentioned in any of the major classifications of mental disorder, despite being used repeatedly in common parlance. So psychopathy is nowhere but everywhere, an elusive will-o'-the-wisp that dances across the stage with a wink and a scowl. People who are psychopathic are the egotists who are always looking to promote their own ends at the expense of others, not caring if they leave chaos and suffering in their wake as they do so. The 'diagnosis' of psychopathy has been given most credence by Robert Hare, a psychologist whose lifelong aim has been to elevate psychopathy into a credible scientific subject.

The main instrument for the diagnosis is the Psychopathy Checklist, or PCL-R,[3] which scores people on 20 items:

- glibness and superficial charm
- grandiose sense of self-worth
- proneness to boredom
- pathological lying
- cunning and manipulative behaviour
- lack of remorse
- shallow feelings (affect)
- callous lack of empathy
- parasitic lifestyle
- current behavioural disturbance
- behavioural problems early in life

- promiscuous sexual behaviour
- absence of long-term goals
- impulsive behaviour
- irresponsibility
- failure to take responsibility for actions
- poor short-term marital relationships
- a history of juvenile delinquency
- recidivism
- 'criminal versatility' (committing crimes in several different areas).

These are more complex to define than the criteria for narcissistic personality disorder and people who use the checklist have to undertake special training before they can administer it. This is quite an experience. Jon Ronson has written about this in his bestselling book *The Psychopath Test*.[4] After three days of training, he claimed to be 'a Bob Hare devotee, bowled over by his discoveries' and 'contemptuous of those people who allowed themselves to be taken in by slick-tongued psychopaths'. *The Psychopath Test* is an entertaining read, but please do not regard it as a work of scholarship, and its subtitle, *A journey through the madness industry*, gives the game away. It skitters across the whole field of mental health in search of funny stories and, in so doing, becomes glib and superficial (it's that court jester again!). To back me up, Robert Hare (Bob to Jon Ronson) does not think much of the book either and describes it as 'frivolous, shallow, and professionally disconcerting'.

But it is also true that it is very difficult to write a book, or even a chapter, on psychopathy. This is because psychopathy covers the whole range of personality disturbance with equal gusto, with Hannibal Lecter at one end of the spectrum (the cannibalistic serial killer described in Thomas Harris's novel *The Silence of the Lambs*[5]) and highly successful businessmen, writers and politicians at the other. Dozens of high-profile people have been labelled as psychopaths and this is because success in many walks of life is measured by the extent to which you can be ruthless in pursuit of your own ends, ignore the feelings of others and experience no remorse when they suffer because of your actions. So, many people are diagnosed as psychopathic after they have committed an appalling act, having never shown evidence before. Stephen Paddock, who committed the most awful mass murder of concertgoers in Las Vegas, was a retired accountant of 64 with no apparent personality disturbance, which his brother, who was almost speechless with incomprehension after the killing, seemed to confirm at interview. Yet, in trying to make sense of his actions, a police spokesman said, 'How do you see into the mind of a psychopath?' If Paddock had died at the age of 63 from a heart attack, would anyone have ever mentioned the word 'psychopathy'? Is a deed a diagnosis?

We must also account for the successful psychopaths we seem to be able to identify all around us who are very different from the serial killers such as Ian Brady, Jack the Ripper and John Christie, who seemed to revel in the suffering of others and have absolutely no feelings for the people they have killed. These other people are shut off from the normal range of human emotions and have a philosophy of life that is completely alien to the rest of us, but the successful ones seem to be completely tuned in.

I will give one example of this detachment from normal thinking and behaviour that characterizes the psychopath who is dangerous. Some years ago, I and colleagues were involved in the assessment of prisoners in what was called the Dangerous and Severe Personality Disorder (DSPD) Programme in England. My wife Helen was assessing one of the people in the new service and finding out what had led him to be involved. Here is the conversation that followed:

> *Helen*: 'I understand you were involved in a murder. What exactly happened?'

Prisoner: 'Well it was like this, doc. This bloke had cheated on me and, because of him, I was banged up in prison for two years. When I got out I had to get my own back and so I went round to his house with a gun to finish him off.'

Helen: 'But I understand he was not the person you killed.'

Prisoner: 'No. It was like this, doc. It was the classic case of the wrong person being in the wrong place at the wrong time. The man who came to the door wasn't the bloke I had come to kill.'

Helen: 'Then why did you kill him?'

Prisoner: 'I had gone round to kill a man so I just had to finish the job. If he hadn't have come to the door I wouldn't have killed him.'

I find this a very chilling account. There is almost an impeccable logic to the series of actions the prisoner describes, but a complete lack of feeling, humanity or any remorse about what had happened. It was as though he had been programmed like a robot to commit a murder, and the fact that the wrong person appeared was just a minor matter. A murder was intended so a murder was done. 'It's as simple as that, doc.'

This is the primitive unthinking world of the psychopath at the end of the spectrum of personality disorder. Here the court jester is dancing with a severed head. Fortunately, this end of the spectrum is very rare.

3

The difference between mental illness and personality disorder

It is February 2008. I am sitting in the Groucho Club in London, famously named after Groucho Marx: 'I would never wanna belong to any club that would have someone like me as a member.' So the Groucho Club does not advertise itself and is hidden away in a corner where only its members, who are in the know, will find it. I am on one of the upper floors waiting for several colleagues who are meeting with me to set up a new journal concerned with personality and mental health. I wait, but my colleagues do not seem to arrive. I go over to another table and see Stephen Fry sitting quietly having a beer. For those who do not know Stephen Fry, and it must be only a tiny proportion of the UK population who don't, he is a celebrity in the broadest sense as he covers every form of entertainment from quiz shows to films, books and drama. To those of us who work in mental health he is also a worthy champion of destigmatization, as he has acknowledged that he has a form of bipolar disorder and has taken the trouble to describe the manifestations of this in coruscating detail, its impact on his life and how he has tackled it.

So, as you might expect in a situation like this after reading the previous chapter and knowing my personality characteristics, I go up to Stephen and say,

'I am meant to be meeting colleagues here to discuss the formation of a new journal focusing on personality disorder, but I seem to have come to the floor for bipolar disorder rather than that for personality?'

Now, Stephen has never seen me before in his life, but he immediately looks at me, unfazed. 'Ah yes,' he says, after the shortest of pauses, 'but it is a moot point where bipolar disorder ends and personality disorder begins.'

Stephen Fry had it exactly right. Why on earth does he know? He is not meant to be a psychiatrist, he has not been properly trained, and yet he has picked up something that many of my professional colleagues have not yet grasped. The boundary line between mental illness and personality disorder is very fuzzy. Indeed, it is so fuzzy that many psychiatrists would like to get rid of the term 'personality disorder' altogether as it simply gets in the way of assessing mental disorder. Others feel that it should be absorbed into other mental disorders and not regarded as special in any way. The funny thing is that people have been trying to get rid of the term 'personality disorder' for years without any success, because when you have defined all your mental illnesses, there is another large group of people who are outside the definition and yet create many problems for themselves and for others. The German psychiatrist, Kurt Schneider, whom we discussed earlier (see p. 18), famously said, 'People with personality disorder suffer from their disorder and cause society to suffer,' which sounds good but isn't all that great as a definition. People with dementia suffer from their disorder and create a great deal of (unintended) suffering to their relatives and society, but this does not make them personality disordered.

There are quite a few differences between personality and its disorder and mental health and its set of disorders. As Stephen Fry suggests, they overlap a little, but at their extremes they are very different. It is worth summarizing these differences.

1 Personality tends to stay reasonably constant throughout life, but mental illness may be very short or, more commonly, comes and goes.
2 Personality is regarded as an intrinsic part of a person, but mental illness is extraneous; there is a time when it is

completely absent and then it seems to infect the person like a typical disease.

3 Most people with personality problems do not want treatment; most people with mental illness do. (There is a big exception to this that we will come to later.)

4 Although there is an obvious overlap, personality problems are mainly concerned with behaviour and mental illness with symptoms (that is, unpleasant feelings that are recognized to be different from normal).

5 People with personality problems, at least in principle, should be able to alter their behaviour. People with mental illness cannot help the way they are, and are often powerless to do anything about their symptoms without help.

When you read this you can get a good idea as to why 'personality disorder' is regarded by most as a nasty couple of words. We can sympathize with people who seem to have real mental diseases, such as schizophrenia or sudden and devastating depression, but when we hear about the damage to people's lives caused by, for example, a personality disorder characterized by extreme aggression, we lose sympathy entirely and start using adjectives like 'evil', 'psycho' (whatever that means) or sadistic. So it is not surprising that, in the past, and still in the present in many countries, personality disorder became, or still is, a diagnosis of exclusion. You could receive a wide range of treatments for mental illness but if you had personality disorder this must be entirely your fault and you should learn how to deal with it yourself before bothering others.

One person whom I have known for over 20 years has a severe personality disorder. Melanie (that is not her name) indulges in a wide range of antisocial behaviour which is at first unrecognized as she talks posh, having been brought up at exclusive private schools. (In England, class barriers still persist and if you talk with an educated accent people will often trust you implicitly.) So, when Melanie was a patient, which she was more often than not, she frequently hailed taxis, gave instructions in her haughty Roedean voice, and, on arrival at the hospital, said she was unable to pay and disappeared.

So we in the hospital had irate taxi-drivers demanding to be paid quite large fares and only receiving sympathy. Melanie also bullied other more vulnerable patients, often in the guise of friendship, and acted as a supplier and purloiner of drugs. She was also highly intelligent and manipulative, and was able to detect both the weak and strong points of other people. Here is the court jester of psychopathy jumping up again. Over the years she has learnt to simulate the symptoms of schizophrenia when she is caught in difficult situations, claiming that the devil is controlling her actions, invading her thoughts and forcing her to do things that she would never contemplate otherwise.

Not surprisingly, many psychiatrists who do not understand the complexities of Melanie have diagnosed her as having schizophrenia and she has accordingly been committed to mental hospitals under the Mental Health Act. But she has never had schizophrenia, and as soon as she sees me – in a hospital, police station, accident and emergency department or at the local shop where she had been shoplifting – she gives up all pretence at being schizophrenic and talks quite normally, as she knows she has been rumbled.

I once had an interesting conversation with her about personality disorder and mental illness. She was trying to convince me that underneath she had a real schizophrenic illness, but it only came out 'at times of stress'. I felt I had to tell her that her real diagnosis was personality disorder. This is how the conversation continued:

'Melanie, you may have a different diagnosis from schizophrenia.'
    'That would be very nice, Peter, but what exactly is it?'
(Melanie likes to use Christian names – she is one for cosy informality.)
    'It's called "personality disorder", Melanie.' (Melanie has

cottoned on that this is not going to be an easy interview, so she is on her guard.)

'What exactly are you getting at, Peter?'

'The way you have been over the last few years makes me think you do not have schizophrenia, as you are much more in control of your behaviour than many think you are.'

'Oh, come off it, Peter. You know I am crazy and just can't stop myself.'

'Ah, but you can, Melanie. Remember how you took that part in our operetta at the Royal College of Psychiatrists' Annual Meeting and were the star of the show in your role as the narrator? You couldn't possibly have done that if you were crazy.'

Melanie now tries a bit of flattery.

'That was because you were there to support me, Peter. I couldn't have done it without your help.'

'When it suits you, Melanie, you can be as well as the rest of us. That's why I think you have a personality disorder, not schizophrenia.'

'Nobody likes to have a personality disorder, so why have you turned against me?'

'I am just trying to be accurate about your diagnosis, Melanie. This is quite important, not least as there are advantages in having personality disorder rather than schizophrenia.'

Melanie laughs raucously.

'And what precisely are these advantages, so I can go out and boast about my new label?'

'This is serious, Melanie. The big advantage of having the diagnosis of personality disorder is that you have much more control over your thinking and behaviour than if you have schizophrenia and, in your case, because you have a lot of antisocial features in your personality, you are not only able to keep it under control but are also likely to be fully recovered by the time you're 50. That doesn't happen very often with schizophrenia.'

'That's very kind of you to tell me, Peter. It is nice to have intelligent conversations with my psychiatrist.'

This conversation may puzzle my readers. This is not the normal way in which doctors talk to their patients and the whole conversation, about a very serious subject, seems to have a mocking quality to it. That is precisely right. I am trying to be serious with Melanie, but she makes sure that the discussion is kept at a trivial or sparring level. She is always playing games. My supposition is that she has been mocking life since she was very young and this manages to protect her from much suffering. What I describe is correct, however odd it may seem.

Melanie's mocking qualities came to the fore in our operetta (about a young Edward Elgar nervously introducing music therapy to the Worcester County Asylum in 1879) and she genuinely was a star as the narrator in our production. She uttered every word in her role as though it was part of a long inside joke, even though, bizarrely, she was detained under Section 25 of the Mental Health Act at the time. The day after she returned to London after this performance she was involved in an examination involving the testing of medical students at St Mary's Hospital in London about their psychiatric knowledge. The medical student quickly got wind of the diagnosis and explained it in detail to the examiner after making his assessment. 'She is totally deluded, believing she has just travelled to Cardiff with Professor Tyrer to take part in a musical production at the Royal College of Psychiatrists and became very upset when I challenged her on this. She would not change her story in the slightest. I believe this to be a delusion as it satisfies the requirements of a delusion, being a false belief held with all the evidence to the contrary. I believe she has paranoid schizophrenia and needs treatment accordingly.' He passed; the examiner did not know the truth.

So you can see how Melanie could persist with the diagnosis of schizophrenia. If you did not know her, you could easily be taken in, and indeed some of my consultant colleagues were so convinced that her behaviour was so unusual that they felt I was being fooled and no other diagnosis could be considered. But in making the case for personality disorder, I made a small mistake when suggesting she would be better by the time she was 50, even though it is generally true that most people with primarily antisocial personality features get better as they get older (see the last chapter of this book).

Some years later, I get an unexpected call on my mobile:

'Hello, Peter. Melanie here. I'm in a rehabilitation unit at Ealing Hospital and would like you to come and discharge me.'

'But I can't do that, Melanie, as I am not the consultant involved in your care now.'

'No, but you are really. You said I would be better by the time I was 50 and it's my fiftieth birthday today.'

This conversation illustrates, in a curious way, why personality disorder is such a stigmatized diagnosis. Here is Melanie, apparently perfectly happy with being labelled with a condition, schizophrenia, that she does not have, even though it involves being treated with unpleasant drugs with a panoply of side effects. It also involves her losing her liberty as she is frequently detained in hospital. So why does she choose this option rather than embrace the lesser evil of personality disorder?

I think it all comes down to responsibility. If you have a personality disorder and do something that harms others, you are regarded as responsible for your actions and therefore can be blamed. If the harm is considerable you can be described as bad, or even evil. If you carry out the same acts under a diagnosis of any severe mental illness, such as schizophrenia or mania, you are regarded as ill and so not responsible. This takes us back to the notion of moral insanity. If you are only unwell within your moral compass, you cannot shake off the judgement that what you do must be known by you to be wrong.

Melanie is not an isolated case, although she is better able to articulate her feelings than most. We have found quite a few people with 'factitious psychosis'. It should really be 'fictitious psychosis', but the adjective 'factitious' is used in psychiatry for a range of disorders that hover between fiction and fact. We call this condition the 'Good Soldier Švejk Syndrome', after the genuinely fictitious eponymous hero of Czech literature. Švejk was a patriotic Czech who created havoc in the Austrian army in the First World War, when the area now covered by the Czech Republic was reluctantly conscripted into supporting Austria and Germany. Švejk behaves as though he is mentally ill and frequently gets admitted to hospital. The uninformed reader has no idea whether he is just a stupid dimwit or a very clever saboteur of the war effort. Ask any Czech citizen and they will give you the same answer.

The 'Good Soldier Švejk Syndrome' thus describes the fictitious manifestations of schizophrenia in people who are using it for their own purposes.[1] Many of these people have personality disorder, which is hardly surprising as no normal person would choose to have such a diagnosis unless there were extremely extenuating circumstances.

Most of this chapter has been concerned with separating personality disorder and mental illness, but, in truth, it is more common for both to exist together. So in the Stephen Fry hinterland between personality disorder and mental illness, we have many people who can show features of both at different times. There are occasions when it is difficult to tell which is which. Some people who are impulsive and great risk-takers indulge in drug or alcohol misuse, and this can quickly change into dependence. So if someone who is rash and impulsive and under the influence of alcohol attacks a policeman, is the behaviour a consequence of alcohol dependence or personality disorder? Similarly, if you are highly anxious and always have been, when you become abnormally shy in company is this part of your personality or is it a diagnosis called social anxiety disorder? If you look at it closely you can see that one may be driving the other. The personality provides the tendency to other mental illness that may become manifest as illness when precipitated by events.

Why is it useful to separate personality disorder from mental illness?

Psychiatrists do not like making the diagnosis of personality disorder, mainly because they think it will be stigmatizing. The same used to be said of mental illness as a whole but it is not a satisfactory solution to push personality disorder under the diagnostic carpet and pretend it doesn't exist. In practice this is what we do. The current world classification of personality disorder (ICD-10) discussed in Chapter 2 is all but ignored by clinicians across the world. They diagnose about 3 per cent of their patients as having personality disorder and, of these, nearly 95 per cent come into the categories of emotionally unstable, borderline type or dissocial (antisocial) or a very silly category called 'mixed' when you cannot make up your mind what is going on.

Yet when we carry out national surveys we find between 5 and 10 per cent of the whole population has a personality disorder, so these two sets of findings cannot both be correct. Research studies also find that approximately 40 to 50 per cent of people who come as in-patients into psychiatric hospitals have a personality disorder. Because the findings in research studies are anonymous the question of stigma does not arise, so I think these higher percentages are more likely to be correct. So if this is the case, the research data are the accurate ones and most mental health professionals (and indeed many in general practice) are seeing people with personality disorders frequently every day.

Because, as we have seen already, personality differs from mental state in a number of ways, it might be considered useful to assess people when they come for psychiatric care for both personality and mental health problems. Interestingly enough, this is what the American classification, DSM, tried to encourage between 1980 and 2013, by having a separate axis of diagnosis for personality disorders. The trouble is, again I think as a consequence of stigma, this double assessment was either rarely tried or, if used, rarely recorded. I, and my colleagues in New Zealand, Giles Newton-Howes and Roger Mulder, feel the loss of this axis will be a loss to psychiatry if it is not reversed.[2]

I hope I can be given a little maudlin self-indulgence at this stage. It is not easy doing research into personality disorders. Your fellow researchers look at you askance for getting involved in a muddy area of mental health, where you are bound to fall over and splash others with ordure, those you treat take the language you use, however much you underplay it, as a form of personal criticism, and your clinical colleagues just think you are bonkers. I have also been likened to Dr Strangelove in my (alleged) obsession with the subject of disordered personality, or perhaps this is because I have a touch of maniacal laughter, and some think I am Harry Potter's nemesis, Lord Voldemort, occupying a dark place from which I emerge from time to time to spread chaos and confusion.

Behind all this apparent genuine criticism mixed with ribaldry is the constant smell of stigma. Time after time I come across colleagues who say that they never use the term 'personality disorder' on the grounds that it is unnecessary. Some more honest ones say they recognize it but prefer never to mention it on the grounds it will cause nothing but trouble and may even poison a therapeutic relationship. Yet these same people will whisper to me confidentially at a cocktail party, 'I know you're interested in this subject, Peter, so don't you think John over there has a personality disorder and I wonder what group he would come into?' I then give a bad-tempered riposte that I am off duty and in any case if they were more diligent in assessing personality in their patients they would have the answer without having to ask me.

Some have suggested that the best way of removing the stigma of the words is to have a change of name. The trouble is that, without a change in attitude, every new name will attract the same level of stigma in time. So we can skip over the word 'disorder' and replace it with 'difficulty', 'disturbance', 'problems in relationships' or 'conflict issues' but personality disorder is always hiding in the background. Perhaps 'personality struc-ture' is a good way of introducing the subject, as it allows the whole spectrum of personality to be considered, it is a fairly neu-tral term.

Examples of the usefulness of separating personality from mental illness

There are many examples of the value of assessing personality status as well as mental illness in clinical practice. Let us take one example of the most common mental illness, depression. When one examines all the studies in which depression and person-ality status have been measured before starting treatment (and these involve over 4,000 service-users) it is found that those who have a pre-existing personality disorder are more than twice as likely to have a poor outcome as those who have no personality disorder.[3] This has nothing to do with the type of treatment; the findings are similar no matter what treatment is given.

But what happens normally in mental health practice? Personality is not assessed, and people are treated with psycho-logical or drug treatments, usually with confident predictions about their success. A minority of these will not improve, and the condition is then labelled as 'chronic' or 'resistant' depres-sion and treated with either higher doses of the psychological or drug treatment, or with a host of additional remedies. How much better it would be if personality was routinely assessed before treatment was given and treatment selected on the basis of both personality and mental state.

Personality and dependence on drugs

There is another example that is worth giving in full as it illus-trates the value of assessing personality status as well as mental illness, and, more particularly, it shows how the attribution of stigma and prejudice has stultified understanding and appreciation of its importance.

As long ago as 1976, I became concerned that patients seemed to be taking benzodiazepines in much greater numbers, and for a much longer time, than might be expected.

To study this further I examined the notes of 287 people referred to a psychiatric clinic from general practice and subsequently published the findings.[4] Of the 287, 220 were taking one or more of 56 different psychotropic drugs at referral, the benzodiazepine diazepam being the most common. Benzodiazepines and barbiturates had been taken for significantly longer than other drugs and there did not seem to be a good reason for this. This made me concerned that dependence might be a problem with benzodiazepines – we already knew that this was true of barbiturates – and so it was worth looking at more closely. This concern was not expressed by others at the time, as benzodiazepines were going through one of their honeymoon phases after official bodies were recommending that barbiturates should no longer be used for the treatment of anxiety and insomnia.

This led to me carrying out further studies and research trials, which showed that a substantial proportion of people (about 40 per cent) suffered significant withdrawal problems when they tried to stop their benzodiazepines. But why was it only 40 per cent? Why was it that the rest could come off their drugs without any real problems? I had a hunch that it might be something to do with their personalities and so included the assessment of personality prior to withdrawal in subsequent studies. The results showed that this hypothesis was supported. Those who had personality disorders or difficulties, especially in the areas that we now call 'negative affectivity' (anxiousness, dependence, moodiness) and 'anankastia' (the old term for obsessionality, rigidity and hyper-conscientiousness), developed withdrawal symptoms.[5] Those who did not have these features could withdraw without difficulty.

Is the importance of personality now accepted in practice?

The answer is no – quite the opposite. I will now introduce a man by the name of Luke, who has written a graphical account of his highly unpleasant experiences with a range of anti-depressant and anti-anxiety drugs, and the withdrawal problems associated with them.[6]

In this account psychiatrists come in for a bit of a pasting. He concludes that there is 'something very wrong at the heart of mainstream psychiatry, which needs to be confronted and overturned before progress can be made'. He described how he had to sue his psychiatrist for prescribing one of the benzodi-azepines, clonazepam, for too long a period, and for putting him through a programme of rapid withdrawal, using a somewhat unusual method. He subsequently had his case settled with a substantial cash payment.

In the course of Luke's description one of the psychiatrists, who had been asked to provide a report about the reasons for Luke's withdrawal symptoms, also comes in for major criticism. Luke writes:

> Much more distressing was the additional diagnosis given to me by one of the expert witnesses, Professor Brown, who – without even meeting me – claimed that I suffer from a personality disorder and this diagnosis would help explain my ongoing symptoms. Brown's argument went as follows: there is research that suggests the personality characteristics are the main drivers of benzodiazepine withdrawal. In his opinion I have a personality disorder (based on a previous doctor's note who wrote that I am a 'workaholic and perfectionistic'); ergo, it is problems with my personality and not the drugs which have caused my withdrawal symptoms.

Luke now gets very angry:

> How dare they first harm me with misprescribed drugs, accept and then deny any responsibility and then conjure up some spurious stigmatizing new diagnosis to trying to wriggle out of the lawsuit? So I decided to dig deeper and discovered that Brown had co-authored four of the five research papers which

he cited in support of the idea that withdrawal symptoms are the result of personality traits. It also turned out that Brown's particular specialism is personality disorders, and his own website states that 'much of his recent work has been concerned with improving and extending the concept of personality disorder.'

Luke has chutzpah and more than his fair share of righteous indignation. A simple reading of this account makes out that Professor Brown is not only incompetent, deceitful and self-serving, forcing his half-baked ideas into areas where they have no place, but is also biased against him because he is acting for the defence.

But just imagine how he would have reacted if Professor Brown was a research biologist who had produced evidence that Luke had a defective gene that had led to his dependence on benzodiazepines. Luke would, very likely, have been impressed by this and would rightly have argued that all people should have this gene test before they started on benzodiazepines. Professor Brown, as a proper scientist, would then be lionized rather than castigated as an incompetent dunderhead who uses his limited abilities to deny and avoid incontrovertible truths.

Of course, personality disorder is not in the same category as a defective gene. Indeed, it is highly unlikely to be understood biologically for very many years, as our personality structure is one of the most complex parts of human behaviour. But this does not mean it does not exist and can be dumped with other spurious diagnoses created mainly for the purpose of swelling the profits of pharmaceutical companies or other discreditable bodies who are not fundamentally interested in the alleviation of human suffering.

Brown's further research has shown that whereas many people could take benzodiazepines for long periods without any problems, others had major difficulty in stopping and many of these had pre-existing personality disturbance. In his subsequent work he has suggested that the minority who have major difficulty in stopping, and have a personality disorder, might be better staying on their drugs in carefully monitored dosage rather than trying to stop them repeatedly. Currently he has several patients who have followed this advice and remain well after many years. Luke might well have been one of them before he started on his campaign, and now is taking no treatment (and, I hope, doing pretty well). The major difficulty for people is the problem of getting repeat prescriptions because many general practitioners are extremely wary of regular prescriptions of benzodiazepines. They understandably do not want to be exposed to legal action along the lines that Luke has described.

It is also perfectly possible for an accurate assessment of personality status to be made from written material without seeing the person. Indeed, it is often much more useful to get contemporaneous accounts of people's personality and behaviour from a lot of different sources than to rely on an interview with somebody who may minimize the impact their personality has on others. Indeed, there is now a scale, developed with the help of a colleague (Lee Anna Clark, from Indiana in the USA) to make these assessments – structured personality assessment from notes and documents (SPAN-DOC) – which has been shown to be of value in practice.[7]

Researchers in mental health do not have the public appeal of popular writers and already this account is getting a little boring. The researchers hunker down in their clinics doing complex research studies, often taking many years, and as much as possible they try to avoid bias and misinterpretation. They then publish in learned journals, read by their colleagues and almost nobody else. Any criticism is dealt with in the correspondence section of the journal. This is usually polite and professional and quite unlike the bile they often get thrown at them in the popular press. A lot of redundant information is published in journals but the best of them have very high standards of probity and science.

But what do the general public read? Not the detailed journal articles or commentaries on them, but popular writings such as those articulated very well by one of the arch-critics of psychiatry, Will Self, who also supports many of the theories put forward by Luke. In a 2013 *Guardian* article, 'Psychiatrists: The drug pushers',[8] Self explores the hypothesis that the current 'epidemic' of mental illness is largely caused by psychiatrists. 'Is the current epidemic of depression and hyperactivity the result of disease-mongering by the psychiatric profession and big pharma?' asks the article.

In it, Self questions the motivations of psychiatrists and explores the view of the profession as a bunch of largely ignorant, drug-pushing doctors who lack common sense and are slaves to the pharmaceutical industry.

In the article, Self reviews a book, *Our Necessary Shadow*,[9] by Tom Burns, Professor of Social Psychiatry at Oxford University, a conscientious and highly committed psychiatrist. While conceding that *Our Necessary Shadow* is a 'lucid, humane and in many ways well-balanced account of the nature and meaning of psychiatry', Self goes on to quote Burns: '"I am convinced psychiatry is a major force for good or I would not have spent my whole adult life in it."' Self continues:

> After all, the alternative – for Burns and for thousands of other psychiatrists – is to accept that in fact their working lives have constituted something of a travesty: either locking up or drugging patients whose diseases are defined not by organic dysfunction but by socially unacceptable behaviours.

This view of psychiatry as a method of social control, with the current 'epidemic' of mental illness being caused by psychiatrists – a blanket statement that should surely be taken as opinion rather than fact – ignores the reality that the profession is trying hard to find the best treatments available and is only too conscious that almost all of them have adverse effects. Self does pay tribute to individual psychiatrists as wise and compassionate individuals in a medical ideology biased towards chemical treatment. If, however, he had turned to the drug treatment of personality disorder (see Chapter 10) I hope he would have understood that much of the apparent 'drug pushing' is a consequence of both doctor and patient struggling together to find solutions to apparently intractable problems, and both have responsibilities in choosing treatments.

It is lucky that Will Self has not turned to personality disorder, because here he would have a field day. If personality disorder was stripped of even 50 per cent of its stigma or had half the public exposure of Will Self, there would be no need for me to write this book and for Stephen Fry to support it.

I hope that the new classification of personality disorder described later will be liberating to both practitioners and service users. If we can take notice of personality as well as symptoms when deciding on treatment we have a much better understanding. There is absolutely no reason why everyone coming to see a general practitioner or psychiatrist, or indeed a psychologist or other mental health professional, should not complete an assessment of personality status (there are now several available), as well as one of mental state. The conversation after this type assessment could be along these lines:

> 'Mrs Smith, you are clearly anxious and depressed at present and it is causing quite a deal of suffering. You also appear to have a mild personality disorder, showing (or your personality structure shows) you are anxiety-prone and more nervous and pernickety than the average person. Because of this combination I am inclined not to prescribe any medication for you at present as you might have difficulty in stopping it in the future. I am therefore going to suggest that we do nothing at present apart from making some adjustments to your lifestyle and circumstances. We can also think about psychological treatment if things do not improve. This does not mean we cannot give you medication, but you need to be aware that you might have to be prepared to take it over a much longer period than you might think, possibly several years.'

You can see that this advice is very different from what would normally be given in practice today. I also appreciate that after a single interview it may be premature to make this recommendation with any degree of firmness. But it does make the point that an early assessment of personality is much better than a later one, when problems may have already developed. If there was better knowledge and awareness of nidotherapy (see Chapter 9 for an explanation) various environmental changes might also be suggested at this point in the interview.

One of the other advantages of doctors knowing something about the personality structure of the people they treat is that it may help them to identify some of the adverse effects of treatment, both drug and psychological types. This subject is very much at its infancy, but if we were able to identify the people who might show highly abnormal and dangerous behaviour after taking a certain treatment, much trouble could be prevented. Drugs that have fundamental effects on what is called 'mood', which covers everything from mild anxiety to severe anger and depression, may occasionally lead to violent and unprovoked aggression or even psychosis. These features do not come out of the blue. They may be hidden in the person and suppressed by normal day-to-day functioning, but there is a danger that they can rampage unprovoked when the normal control mechanisms are switched off.

For many years, I and like-minded colleagues have argued that some sort of assessment of personality should be made with every person seen for the first time. It is a good way of getting to know what is really going on. It makes a two-dimensional assessment into a three-dimensional one. A personality assessment is also greatly appreciated by people if it is done in the right way. 'I know where I am with that doctor. He tells it like it is and it's made me think about myself in a different way.' If we do not assess personality at all we run into the trap of treating syndromes, not people. Of course this makes the initial interview a little longer but it pays off in the long run.

If we do not assess personality in mental health evaluation we just become assessors of problems. One of the sad consequences of excessive pressures on health services is the focus on statutory clinical responsibility. This is heavily influenced by risk. So a cardiologist who sees people who present with symptoms such as tightness in the chest, palpitations and chest pain is charged with deciding if cardiac disease is the cause of these symptoms. If the cardiologist fails to identify cardiac disease when this is present he or she is not only criticized but also can be sued if the delay in diagnosis was responsible for further problems, particularly sudden death.

All this is understandable, but more than two-thirds of people who present with these symptoms do not have any cardiac disease but have abnormal health anxiety (that is, they worry unduly about their health and fear they have a much more serious condition than the doctor has diagnosed). The cardiologist is not trained in the management of health anxiety, or indeed any other form of mental disorder, so the only thing that can be offered is reassurance. This is not only ineffective but also counterproductive and the right way forward is to provide a simple form of psychological therapy, ideally given by nurses in the clinic, that has been shown to have long-lasting benefit.[10]

A very similar situation occurs in the average psychiatric clinic when someone presents with recurrent depression or anxiety. Once these problems recur frequently the first thing that should be considered is the personality status of the person. This is in no way a criticism of the person, but these recurrent disorders do not just happen out of the blue; they are usually a direct consequence of a trigger-linked personality disturbance.[11] If we take this into account by making a good assessment of personality we can avoid long periods of overtreatment or the despairing conclusion that the person is 'treatment resistant'.

So my advice to people who need to go to health professionals with any problem linked to mental health is to be spontaneous in discussing your personality when it comes to treatment. If a GP offers to give you a tranquillizing drug such as diazepam 'for a few days', it is worthwhile interjecting and saying (if it is true), 'I've always been more anxious than other people and I think I may have difficulty in stopping this drug. Is there anything else you can recommend?' You are not disclosing weakness by mentioning these personality characteristics; you are protecting yourself.

4

Politics and personality

It is October 2007. I am presenting the Milroy Lecture at the Royal College of Physicians in London on the subject of personality disorder. This is somewhat nerve-wracking, as no psychiatrist has given this lecture before and I do not want to let my branch of the profession down. The Royal College of Physicians is an imposing building on the edge of Regents Park in London that has rightly won many awards for its architecture. I arrive in time and try to find a side entrance to slink into, but none is available. I take a deep breath and go through the main glass doors where the staff are waiting to greet me and the other visitors.

So what am I doing at the Royal College of Physicians? The Milroy Lecture was endowed by Gavin Milroy in 1877 to provide an annual lecture on 'state medicine and public hygiene'. Nowadays, but probably not in 1877, mental illness comes within the ambit of this broad subject. The title of my lecture is 'Personality disorder and public mental health' and it was necessary to justify this in the application.

Milroy, in his notes about the possible subjects of the lecture, had given me an entry door. He suggested that public mental health included the Cachexiae, or 'chronic constitutional diseases which consist of the depraved state of the whole or a considerable part of the habit of the body, without any primary pyrexia or neurosis combined with that state'. Once you make allowances for the archaic and slightly offensive Victorian language, personality disorder could be shoe-horned into this group.

So I duly went to join my medical colleagues, rather surprised to find that my main audience was a sea of consultant physicians interspersed with only a few of my friends from mental health. The subject of my talk was clearly far removed from the main interests of the audience, as it quickly became apparent that most of them were attending a postgraduate course in medicine. They only came to my talk because it was a suitable interlude in their planned programme. I was aware that it was going to be hard to engage them, so added a bit of entertainment and a few jokes, even though my main message was that personality and its associated disorders, however they were described, were important to every doctor, in every speciality, and could not be ignored.

I finished and the friendly and engaging President of the College, Ian Gilmore, who has done a lot for psychiatry by taking on the entrenched interests of the alcohol industry in promoting preventative measures to reduce alcoholism, turned to the audience for questions. There was a short silence. Then, after a slight sniggering at the side of the lecture theatre, came the first question: 'Who has the more serious personality disorder, Tony Blair or Gordon Brown?'

Of course, this was 2007, and today Boris Johnson, Donald Trump and Michael Gove would probably be substitute names, but I was deflated. I should have expected this type of question – it is always being asked of me by people I meet in social settings – but I was expecting my educational talk to raise the tone to a higher plane. I wanted to hear, 'What can I do for the people I see in my cardiology practice with personality disorder, I am sure there are a lot of them?' or, at least, 'If I think someone has a personality disorder how should I disclose my suspicions to them or should I just keep quiet?' No, it was just an ideal opportunity for everyone to indulge in a favourite pastime, 'Stick a personality label on your favourite politician'.

The question was probably meant to be a joke, but at another level it was deadly serious. Many people dislike Tony Blair and Gordon Brown for a variety of reasons and, as we have already established that many of the people psychiatrists dislike are labelled as personality disordered, it should not be too much of a surprise that the general public adopt the same strategy. But the classification of personality disorder is meant to be a scientific subject, so to use it indiscriminately in this way is tantamount to abuse. I have never met Tony Blair or Gordon Brown, but from my knowledge of them, both negative and positive, it is enough for me to say that they do not have any degree of pathology that could be properly described as significant personality disorder.

This is not an isolated example. In the course of writing this chapter I have been asked by several media outlets to make a comment on a recent 'investigation' that has concluded Donald Trump, the US President, has narcissistic personality disorder. (Since then, everybody else seems to be saying it too – but he would call it 'fake news' without elaboration.) I refused to respond, as taking part in the exercise would only detract from the whole purpose of this book. Personality disorder and all elements of personality dysfunction are complex and serious subjects that cannot be condensed into a few stupid sound bites and what many would pass off as jokes despite their serious implications.

So why is it that so many politicians seem to attract the label of personality disorder? Is it an accurate impression or is there another explanation? To answer this I will compare the personalities of Donald Trump (a presumed assessment as I have never met him) and Hamish, my short-haired black and white-pawed cat.

Both of them seem to have remarkably similar personalities. Hamish, who has been described earlier, is self-opinionated and attention-seeking, walking into a room with strangers with a loud informative miaow ('Here am I and you had better take notice of me'). He then parades up and down like a model on a catwalk (very appropriately named). This usually has the desired effect of creating greater interest, but if it does not he jumps on people's laps and nuzzles people's hands to be stroked so he can generate reciprocal affection. If he does not get the response he needs he harasses people until he is satisfied, often giving them a nip in the process, and then walks out with his tail in the air. Donald Trump behaves in the same way. He has to be noticed and command attention. If he is thwarted he reacts angrily. He demands affection and does not like finishing an interaction until he gets it. Like Hamish, he never has any regrets about his behaviour.

So why is it that we can regard Hamish as 'a character' and Donald Trump, at least in many people's eyes, as someone suffering from a personality disorder? Both of them can be regarded without much contradiction as psychopathic, but this is a very elastic term, as we have already observed. They are both promoting themselves, often at the expense of others (poor Haggis, the twin of Hamish, always gets pushed aside by his brother), and both are grossly egocentric. There are two differences that stand out apart from the obvious one of communication: predictability and inconsistency.

Politicians are predictably inconsistent: they promise many things that cannot be delivered, then have to change their minds while pretending they have not and sometimes contradict themselves absolutely. 'Black is white; they both look black in the dark.' We, the general public, are no different, in that we can promise, pledge, cheat, lie and deceive just as readily as the smooth politicians of this world. The difference is that politicians make their promises in public to large groups of people and, to get through to the voters, have to overstate their case. As a consequence, a politician will virtually always let the people down. And, as their promises could, if implemented, have a big effect on people's lives, the let-down can be a major bump. As a consequence, it could be argued that politicians really do qualify for our definition of personality disorder, because they create interpersonal dysfunction and conflict.

This is not really fair, as this is not conflict through direct contact with the people they upset. But, because politicians invade the airwaves and almost every other media outlet nowadays, they appear to be people we know very well, so personal animosity or support is a component of their relationship with us. This is now being reinforced greatly by social media.

So when Donald Trump tweets his misspellings to the world about his great achievements in making America great again or lambasts the media for broadcasting fake news (that is, anything not supporting the Trumpian line), he is inviting us to assess his personality just as much as we do the loquacious neighbour next door. Everybody becomes a social psychologist, tossing around personality labels like confetti. So here are some of the conclusions of these armchair commentators: Trump is a habitual psychopath (glib promises and habitual lying), narcissistic (excessively self-important, massive self-entitlement, always insists he is right), borderline (alternating between good-natured charm and downright hostility), histrionic (always demanding to be the centre of attention), paranoid (finding slights in any form of comment that is less than adulatory) and antisocial (threatening and intimidating others, often with violent undertones).

These suggest he must have a severe personality disorder, but, apart from illustrating yet again that these labels are of limited scientific value, they also fail to consider that these alleged personality features may be part of the Donald Trump master plan. Trump did not become President of the United States by accident. He had a strategy that turned out to be highly successful. He rubbished all the other candidates as though they were apprentices on his game show; he appealed to the core emotions of a substantial part of the US electorate; and he attacked the whole system of government that had lost contact with the electorate.

'Draining the swamp', one of the rallying calls in his election campaign, was a very clever way of tuning into the anger that many people felt. Believing they had been let down by politicians and the machinery of government, they were prepared to make a leap into the unknown.

So we may suspect that Donald Trump has a personality disorder, especially when he seems to wear his more negative personality traits on his sleeve. But we have to acknowledge that much of his behaviour that we regard as outrageous, and his bizarre public pronouncements, is organized, even if only at an emotional level. If we take his pronouncements as a true reflection of his personality, as indeed we can with some confidence with most people without ever seeing them if we have access to records about them,[1] we would conclude he had at least a moderate degree of personality disorder. Tom Coburn, an ex-Republican senator, has explicitly stated this. But what if these apparently random interjections of a disturbed adolescent are part of a political strategy that to date has been highly successful (whether or not it is in the long term)? My colleague Allen Frances goes even further in saying that Donald Trump does not have a personality disorder. In his view, Trump may be supremely unqualified to be president 'by habitual dishonesty, bullying bravado, bloviating ignorance, blustery braggadocio, angry vengefulness, petty pique, impulsive unpredictability, tyrannical temper, fiscal irresponsibility, imperial ambitions, constitutional indifference, racism, sexism, minority hatred and divisiveness', but this does not constitute personality disorder.[2] I would not be so generous in agreeing with Allen, who nonetheless has a fine line in vitriol. I suspect that Donald Trump in his private life has caused significant long-term distress to others and so may qualify for significant personality abnormality, but his public pronouncements alone do not confirm this. People may also be influenced by the slang expression of his name – a gaseous eruption full of sound and fury but signifying nothing apart from minor internal combustion.

Donald Trump may be an exception among politicians, not least as he claims not to be a politician at all, but he is now making political decisions, or at least they appear to be so even if he seems to be acting in vaudeville. Such decisions can never please everybody – such decisions never will – and in reacting to them, we, the public, exposed to this massive blast of ego, are forced to examine him, rather obliquely, in character form, just as we would if the dinosaur Tyrannosaurus Rex suddenly burst into the twenty-first century. We would be put off a little by that enormous head and rows of pointed teeth, but after finding out what he had for breakfast, we would be equally keen to know what pleased him, what made him angry, what his behaviour was like towards his tyrannosauric children and how he interacted with other animals. So, without knowing much about a politician's personality, we ask the same sort of questions that researchers do when making personality assessments: Can I believe what he says? Is that smile sincere or artificial? Is he really as angry as he sounds? Does he really behave like that in private? Is he really as crazy as he sounds or is this just for show?

This need to get close to the persona, the essential element of inner personality, is particularly true when a politician tugs at our emotions. If what he or she says resonates with our underlying feelings, it is much easier to regard many of the other statements that are expressed as flashes of insight into our own psychology rather than the manoeuvrings of a con artist.

But there are other reasons why politicians might be more likely to be regarded as personality disordered than the rest of us. They have great influence over our lives and can make or destroy large numbers of people by their actions. Lord David Owen was Foreign Secretary in the Labour Government in the UK in the 1970s, and leader of the now redundant Social Democratic Party in the 1980s, but before then he was briefly a psychiatrist who taught me as a medical student. He has always kept his medical interest alive and has recently identified what he regards as an acquired personality disorder called the 'hubris syndrome', which is particularly prevalent among politicians but which is also found among others who wield great power, whether they be dictators, royal despots or captains of industry.[3]

David Owen's reasoning goes like this. When leaders are first elected, crowned or force themselves to the top of any big hierarchy, they listen to people carefully, make decisions based more or less on consensus, and are balanced in their interaction with others. (All right, we all know Donald Trump is an exception.) Once they have been in their powerful positions for many years, they cease to listen, become arrogant and feel that only they know the answers to important questions, then act unilaterally without thinking about the consequences. He cites Margaret Thatcher, George Bush and Tony Blair among others who have the syndrome, and points to its potential dangers – the Iraq War being a good example.

I cannot buy this as a personality disorder. There are some very good examples of dictators who were undoubtedly personality disordered. Adolf Hitler and Joseph Stalin come into this category, as does one of the Anglo-French sovereigns, King John. John has always interested me, so much so that I have written a play about his last days when, rather late in the day, he realized he was far from divine.[4] He failed miserably as a king because he was petty, spiteful and vindictive, and this was true from the moment he was crowned in 1199. He had a full dose of hubris, self-importance and vanity from the start, and Hitler and Stalin were little different. They did not need power to show their arrogance, deceit and brutality. The phenomenon that David Owen describes is better defined as the Canute Conundrum, the tendency of all rulers to surround themselves with acolytes and yes-men, to stop listening to those who disagree on key issues, and become so tied up in a cocoon of certainty separated from the world that they end up marooned.

King Canute was aware of this when he had to silence the sycophantic praise of his courtiers. 'Do you believe that I have the power to control the tides?' 'Yes, indeed, Your Highness.' 'Then take me down to the sea and I will test whether you are right.' After he had failed to reverse the direction of the incoming tide by sitting in a chair at the water's edge and demanding it to retreat unsuccessfully, in what could have been an early Monty Python sketch – 'Turn back, you naughty frothy wave number four from the back, I order you' – I hope he got a little more honesty from his staff. But I suspect he did not; the flattery continued in more subtle form. Hubris goes with great success in every walk of life. 'We are more famous than Jesus now', said John Lennon in a moment of crass silliness. 'God created the world; I organized it', claimed the great classifier of living things, Linnaeus. 'Give me a museum and I'll fill it', said Pablo Picasso, probably correctly. But it just needs a little bad fortune to come along for the hubris to be modified and for common sense to take over.

We come across this phenomenon very often in daily life. After sudden success we so often hear the unwise boast, the belittling of others, the transparent false modesty, and the harshness of brazen superiority. These grate and annoy, but most often they are recognized as temporary and found to be so. They are not the stuff of pathology.

So when we get annoyed with politicians, rail at their ignorance or stupidity, or rant that they have lost touch with the real world even though they claim to represent it, it is better to recognize these feelings as facets of disagreement, not innate mental pathology. And while we may not be able to stop introducing personality labels such as narcissistic, histrionic or psychopathic in the descriptions of their behaviour, these must not be regarded necessarily as part of underlying personality; they are just descriptions of human behaviour.

Extending these to personality disorder is just a lazy way of justifying our own political views. We should also avoid the use of other labels such as 'schizophrenic' or 'bipolar', as their use does a disservice to the people who really do have these disorders and merit greater respect for living with them. And we need to finish the comparison with Hamish, my cat. He makes no attempt to hide his views, to disguise his selfishness, to demand what he wants or to ignore the wishes of others, but, unlike politicians, he is utterly reliable and consistent and makes it very clear that he is pleased with his lot and has no desire to change the world.

5

When is personality disorder formed?

I am 11 years old. It is the autumn of my first term at my secondary school. We are all slightly wary of each other, but I have the advantage of some familiarity as I am in the same class as my identical twin brother. It is just after 4.30 p.m. and classes have finished for the day. The class monitor, another 11-year-old whom we will call Francis, looks a little nervous. He feels it is time for everyone to go home and says so. It is really unnecessary for him to do this, but he is taking his duties very seriously, and, without realizing it, is becoming a bit irritating.

Nobody takes any notice of his suggestion, so he repeats it. Several other boys say pointedly, 'We are staying.' The tension is beginning to rise in the room and Francis looks more nervous.

'Well, I don't know about you but I'm going to go home now,' he says, and makes a move towards the door.

Three other boys, apparently spontaneously, block his path and say coolly and menacingly, 'No, Francis, it is not time for you to go home yet. You are going to have to stay.'

We other boys, including my brother and me, are fascinated by this interchange but do not intervene.

'No, Francis,' says the apparent ringleader, 'you are not going home. In fact, you are probably never going home.'

Francis is now sweating. 'You have to let me go; you have no right to keep me here.' His voice is getting shrill; he is clearly terrified.

'You sit down over there and stop making a fuss, because – you-are-staying-here.'

Eventually Francis is allowed to leave, but only after he is reduced to tears and crawling on the floor asking for mercy. The ringleader smiles with satisfaction at his two co-conspirators and opens the door. We all leave, Francis blubbering and red-faced, many of us as onlookers feeling ashamed for allowing this to happen and doing nothing about it. The next day, as we all expected, Francis asks to be relieved of his post as class monitor.

This, of course, is classic bullying, but a little more sophisticated than most. Bullies often grow up to be similar in adult life; they like intimidating and controlling others, and many of them have clear personality problems that persist throughout their lives. But when I met the ringleader of this episode many years later, he was a fine upstanding citizen working in the civil service and could not remember anything about this episode when I tried to remind him.

I tell this story because it explains one of the real difficulties in describing and, I hesitate to use the word, 'labelling' personality disorder. Several facts are now well known, accurate and yet contradictory.

1 Personality disorder does not develop in adult life; it is formed in childhood.
2 Genetic and environmental factors influence personality development roughly equally.
3 Most of the fundamental features of personality are recognizable in childhood.
4 When there is abuse or neglect in childhood personality disorder is more likely to develop.

Personality disorder is formed in childhood

One of the curious things about the current classification of personality disorder is that it is only made formally when a person has reached the age of 18. This is particularly odd when it has been known for many years that personality development takes place in the early years of life. It is even possible to identify personality characteristics in infants. In one of the best-known studies, Jerome Kagan, a professor of psychology at Harvard University, showed that infants at the age of four months could be separated by their personality characteristics. Babies that responded to new stimuli such as different voices and sounds, a new toy or even a new smell could be separated into what were called 'high reactors' and 'low reactors'. Low reactors were curious and often interested in these new experiences and showed no evidence of alarm. High reactors, about 10 per cent of infants, were distressed, cried and flailed their arms and legs, and appeared to be overwhelmed by the changes in the environment. Kagan formulated the hypothesis that these children were more likely to develop into adults with anxious and inhibited personalities,[1] and further research showed this was indeed the case.

Once babies have grown into toddlers there is even better identification of two broad groups of personality – rather clumsily called 'externalizers' and 'internalizers'. Externalizers appear to be understimulated and need or demand input from people or external events, whereas internalizers appear to be overstimulated and tend to be withdrawn or be satisfied by their own thoughts and interests. Later in childhood, and especially at school, the extremes of externalization and internalization are described as disorders. External behaviour problems include bullying, risky behaviour, drug-taking, and problems in concentration. Internal behaviour problems include isolation at school, anxiety, lack of self-confidence, being victims of bullying, and social withdrawal. Sometimes internal and external problems can occur together.

Because there is reluctance to identify personality problems in childhood, there is a tendency to give these disorders separate diagnostic labels. So pupils with these behaviour problems can be readily given diagnoses of attention deficit hyperactivity disorder (ADHD), autistic spectrum disorder (ASD) and Asperger's syndrome. These conditions undoubtedly exist, but their diagnoses have been widely criticized for being overused. Many of the pupils so diagnosed are showing mild evidence of personality disturbance, which may or may not persist, but it is an overreaction to give them a childhood diagnostic label. One of the major deficiencies of our current attitudes, as well as our services in child and adolescent mental health, is the failure to provide intervention early for these problems when personality is still under development and has a greater chance of being modified. Teachers have a major role in identifying pupils at risk and need more training here.

Genetic and environmental factors influence personality development roughly equally

There have been dozens of studies examining the genetics of personality disorder. They all come up with the same results. Half of the influences creating personality disorder are genetic, the other half are environmental.[2] At various times people have claimed otherwise with absolute statements – 'Some people are just born evil', 'All those with personality disorder have suffered abuse as children' – but the evidence contradicts this. The difficulty comes in allocating each half. In particular, borderline personality disorder – about which more later – has been heavily studied as its features are more prominent than many others in adolescence and early adult life. There is no doubt that some people who develop the up-and-down, excoriating awful mood swings and personal conflicts created by this disorder have suffered enormously in childhood and their problems seem to develop directly from these experiences. But there are others who go through the same experiences and come out relatively unscathed. There is even a word borrowed to describe the positive effects of such experiences – steeling, best described as reinforcement through adversity.

Most of the fundamental features of personality are recognizable in childhood

I have seen Francis (the boy who was bullied) and his bullying counterpart several times recently. I was only reminded of the classroom episode by seeing them together. Although everything about them on the surface was different, they were essentially the same people, with their intrinsic vulnerabilities, as they had been 55 years earlier. The teasing and mildly sadistic tendencies of one, and the nervous reactions of the other, could be identified quite easily.

So although personality is not fully formed until later in adolescence, many of the features are identifiable much earlier in life, as found in Jerome Kagan's studies. Some people make a distinction between temperament and personality, with temperament being a more basic structure on which personality is developed. This may be just playing with words, but what is important is that the building blocks of personality are all there at a very early age.

This is particularly important with the group of personalities that can collectively be called antisocial. Young people who are aggressive, disruptive, always challenging authority (oppositional) and impulsively dangerous are given the label – it is really too vague to be called a diagnosis – of conduct disorder. Some children with conduct disorder are just naughty and boisterous, or if aggressive are copying others in deprived environments. Others have been identified as 'callous and unemotional',[3] and these may be the ones who become severely antisocial and dangerous in adult life. But we do not yet know if this is the case, as we need long-term follow-up studies to find out if callous and unemotional children become equally callous and unemotional adults and whether these features persist into old age. These studies are difficult to carry out, but not impossible.

What is important is to be able to diagnose, or at least have some form of tagging, those who have abnormal personality features in childhood and adolescence, and to intervene if needed long before adulthood is reached. The new classification of personality disorder will allow a diagnosis of 'personality disorder in development' to be made in adolescence. Some people, especially professionals in child and adolescent psychiatry, abhor the prospect of this as the premature attachment of dangerous 'labelling', but if we can destigmatize personality abnormality more effectively this should not be a bar. One of the positive aspects about personality abnormality in adolescence compared with adult life is that at younger ages the chances of the disorder persisting are so much less than when it is diagnosed later. This explains the more ambiguous description of 'personality disorder in development'.

When there is abuse or neglect in childhood, personality disorder is more likely to develop

In recent years we have been made increasingly aware of the extent of childhood abuse in our society. No matter where you look, whether it is in people's homes, schools, hospitals, churches or other institutions, when the stones of cover are lifted we find abuse underneath, and this is sadly almost universal. If this abuse was taken away completely – a fanciful idea, I grant you – the mental health of the population would improve more dramatically than any of the treatments we have for mental disorder, as every psychiatric condition has been found to be much more frequent in those who have been abused.

Although abuse has a marked influence on the development of personality disorders it is sometimes difficult to disentangle these disorders from their effects on other mental conditions such as anxiety, depression, eating disorders, schizophrenia, bipolar disorder, obsessive-compulsive disorder, ADHD and phobias. The most striking association is found with borderline disorder discussed more fully in the next chapter. Some people have gone so far as to say that borderline personality disorder is another form of post-traumatic stress disorder, with many of the features of the condition being delayed for several years.

So why is it, when abuse in childhood has such a marked influence in the generation of all personality disorders, that those with the borderline disorder get so much more attention than those in other groups? The answer seems to be that it is easier to explain. There has been a great deal of interest in the ways in which infants and young children develop relationships with adults as they grow. This has led to an expanding area of understanding known as attachment theory.

Attachment theory sometimes sounds more complicated than it is, but its basis is quite straightforward. An English psychiatrist and psychoanalyst, John Bowlby, first described this in the 1950s,[4] and his colleague Mary Ainsworth developed it further. Bowlby noted from keen observation that infant development is very dependent on the relationship with the mother or, if another person takes this role, the primary care-giver. (Bowlby himself described his nanny as his primary care-giver as he saw little of his mother when very young.) If the baby's relationship with this person was caring, warm and close, then later development was positive and healthy. If the relationship was poor or absent, subsequent development was likely to be distorted. There were four types of attachment that were identified: secure attachment, anxious-avoidant, anxious-ambivalent and avoidant attachment, and those with no clear links were 'disorganized' attachments.

Secure attachment was concluded to be the ideal with a good care-giver and this promotes normal development. When parenting is inconsistent the child is not sure how to react. Anxious-ambivalent attachment occurs when a closer relationship is desired but not achieved, leading to excessive dependence and alarm when the child is separated. Other (anxious-avoidant) children who feel that getting a better relationship is not worth the candle opt out by being wary and independent and forge their own paths. Disorganized attachment occurs when no meaningful relationship is established at all. Bowlby predicted, not always correctly as so many other influences come into play, that personality disorder only developed in adult life when secure attachment was not achieved in the first 30 months of life. Dependent, antisocial and detached personalities were natural consequences of anxious-ambivalent, disorganized and anxious-avoidant attachments. Subsequent researchers, headed by Peter Fonagy, have suggested that this is more complex but that these maladaptive attachments are largely responsible for the development of borderline personality disorder.[5]

Bowlby developed his theory from studying other animals as well as humans, and argued that good parenting was of major evolutionary importance. You can readily see the consequences of abuse in the maltreatment of pets. A puppy or kitten is naturally playful and engages well with hunt and chase and similar games. But these young animals are highly vulnerable, and if kicked, derided and threatened they become wary, detached and cautious about their future relationships with these unreliable humans. Even if the abuse only lasts for a short time the personality of the dog or cat can be permanently changed. Scars have formed and these are never completely eradicated.

So an abused child also becomes wary, detached and very cautious in dealing with adults. Unfortunately, all too often, the bullied then become bullies as they pass through childhood, as though the exercise of power somehow compensates for the powerlessness they experienced only a short time ago. If people have no positive feelings towards you it is very difficult for you to have positive feelings for them, and it is easy for anger at the way you have been treated to turn towards revenge. Similarly, a rejected child who is searching for love and affection that never seems to arrive, clings on to relationships in later life and becomes overdependent.

These are not simple cause-and-effect relationships, so too much must not be read into them. But they explain why it is so important to have the option of diagnosing 'personality disorder in development' when assessing younger people. If we can intervene earlier in life when things are going astray we are likely to have much better success at reversing these negative changes than if we wait until adult life. I say this with some feeling, because in 1980 I was giving a talk at a psychiatric meeting and defending the official decision to make the diagnosis of personality disorder at the age of 18 and no earlier. John Bowlby was in the audience. He leapt up and shouted, 'That is a political decision, not a scientific one.' He was absolutely right, and to my shame I have to admit I was completely wrong.

6

The new classification

The new classification of personality disorders is now almost upon us, and will be introduced within the next two years. The definitions that are written below should not be regarded as final; changes are bound to be made, but the essentials are the same, and the current form is shown here and elsewhere.[1]

The words in psychiatric definitions are dry and impersonal, and need to be lubricated by the oil of illustrations to bring them to life and meaning. In reading these definitions we need to be reminded that they cover the whole spectrum of personality, and that every person on the planet is on this spectrum, admittedly including a large number who are only defined by exclusion, as there is no definition of normal personality. You may rightly say that these descriptions are inadequate to describe the subtlety and range of personality across the population, but they do not attempt this task. The descriptions are only there to act as anchor points on the spectrum, milestones on the long personality road from smooth travel to rocky disintegration. They are also only there for use by clinicians (doctors, psychologists and a range of other mental health professionals), not for the general public, but I think it is only right for all to know what they are and what they mean.

They also contain a great deal of jargon, a word I define as 'an attempt to hide the real meaning of words from all but a selected few'. Some translation and elucidation of jargon is therefore needed frequently.

The following are the requirements for the diagnosis of a personality disorder.

Essential (required) features

- An enduring disturbance in how an individual experiences and interprets the self, others and the world, shown by maladaptive patterns of cognition, emotional experience, emotional expression and behaviour.
- These maladaptive patterns are mostly inflexible and are associated with significant problems in psychosocial functioning that are particularly evident in interpersonal relationships.
- The disturbance is manifest across a range of personal and social situations (that is, it is not limited to specific relationships or situations).
- The disturbance is moderately stable over time and is of long duration. Personality disorder typically has its first manifestations in adolescence and is clearly evident in young adult life.
- These patterns of behaviour are significantly different from the person's cultural expectations.

The definition also includes late-onset personality disorder and personality disorder in development.

All the features for the diagnosis of personality disorder are met for these disorders except for the age at which it becomes apparent. In late-onset personality disorder the essential features only become manifest after the age of 25 and have been persistent for at least two years. The diagnosis of personality disorder in development can also be made if the essential features have been present for at least two years but the person has not reached the age of 18.

Where do domains come in?

The domains of personality have already been discussed. The five types are difficult to remember as they use unfamiliar words. A bit of translation is needed.

Anankastic domain 'Anankastic' is a term that has been used in European psychiatry for over 100 years. It derives from a Greek word incorporating 'compulsion' and 'need' and could easily be translated as 'obsessional'. This is easily recognizable. People in this domain are meticulous, fussy, rigid and excessively conscientious, wishing to do everything their own way and often needing to be in control.

Detached domain This is the easiest one, as it is almost self-explanatory. People with this characteristic are one or two steps away from society. They do not mix easily with people, prefer their own company to that of others, and are pretty poor at 'reading' those around them. Reading people is much more difficult than reading text. The clues are not in the writing, but in body language, tone and attitude, and those who are detached tend to ignore or misread them. As a consequence they create upset without really understanding why.

Dissocial domain Many prefer the word 'antisocial' to 'dissocial'. The reason for not using 'antisocial' is that there are many more ways of upsetting society in its many forms apart from the anti-group. Many who are dissocial appear to be prosocial in their behaviour. This particularly applies to the overused word 'psychopath'. Many people satisfying the umbrella-like term of psychopathy do very well in life by a combination of manipulation, greed and enterprise, but in promoting themselves they bring others with them and, at least at first, can be regarded as successful. (Yet again the conversation comes round to Donald Trump, but we will resist.)

Negative affective domain This is the unfortunately worded term for nervous, miserable and angry emotions. 'Affect' is the technical word for 'mood', but it is really unnecessary. 'How does affect affect people?' runs the question, but, of course, it is meaningless. Negative affects are what used to be called neuroses, but now that the word neurotic is regarded as a term of criticism, we have to retreat into the polysyllabic neutrality of negative affectivity. If you think of this domain as covering a range of unpleasant feelings and emotions we would prefer not to have, you have the gist.

Disinhibited domain The tendency to act without thinking too much, then regret it afterwards is pretty universal, but people in this domain are experts at it and, as a consequence, create havoc in their own lives and those of others. This characteristic can show itself in many different areas – finance, sex, occupation and spare time – and the consequences are debt, unwanted pregnancy, sexually transmitted diseases, unemployment and broken bones. In personal relationships, disinhibition can also be very damaging. Anne Boleyn lost her head by making an inappropriate disinhibited comment to a poor young man, implying that she could be his wife. He lost his head too and all he did was to listen.

As emphasized earlier, domains are not, and never can be, diagnoses in their own right. They qualify the level of severity but do not replace it. So it is perfectly possible to have mild degrees of any of these domain features, but if the severity level is the bottom category of 'normal' they can all be ignored. What does tend to happen, and it fits in with what can be called the 'pond ripple' analogy, is that when the severity level is moderate or severe, the domain ripples crash into each other and become more frequent, so that it is rare for someone with a severe personality disorder to have problems in only one domain.

To stop this getting too complicated here are some illustrations of people on the severity spectrum. Everybody is on this spectrum, so you can decide on your position as you read the examples. 'I am like none of these,' you might say when you get to the end, but you are and, if you doubt it, ask someone whom you know really well who is prepared to speak honestly about you without favour, and check again.

Normal personality

There is no definition of a 'normal personality' in any formal classification – it is just the absence of personality abnormality. Would you like to be like my example?

The setting is Tree Court, Gonville and Caius College, Cambridge, 1959. A new term has started at this Cambridge college and little knots of undergraduates are meeting, introducing themselves somewhat hesitantly, like nervous actors preparing for the first night of a play. But one knot is bigger than the others and a young man in the middle is the focus of attention and chatter. It is David Frost, in his element as entertainer and excitement generator. Many in his position might be a little less confident, as last term he failed his first-year exams and only a dramatic display of contrition and impassioned pleas for clemency prevented his expulsion from the college.

But they were right to keep him on. Even though his academic performance was mediocre, his performances at the Cambridge Footlights revue and his ability to attract others of high calibre to student publications made him a man to watch and before long his effortless 'rise without trace' led him into the television spotlight. No nerves in front of the camera for him. Here was a willing aid, 'talking to the camera seemed the most natural thing in the world'. His skill as a facilitator and interviewer eventually led to his greatest triumph: the interviews with Richard Nixon over Watergate, which were first treated as a joke by Nixon's advisers but led dramatically to the sad confession of a broken man, 'I let the American people down.'

So why do I regard David Frost as having a normal personality? It is because he had no smidgeon of the characteristics of personality difficulty defined above. People often said he was impossible to dislike, even if he dissected them in television interviews. This was because he was a human chameleon; he adjusted himself exactly to the persona of the person he was interviewing, yet gave no indication of his own views and therefore came over as entirely without bias. He was a robotic empathizer, insistingly probing in a clinical forensic examination of the person in front of him, with the ability to shift course immediately if the response demanded it.

In other settings he used these skills to bring out the best in people. Sheila Hancock has commented in her diaries how much she felt let down when meeting celebrities. They were just boring and plain ordinary. But David was able to bring out the best in everyone, so they flocked to see him whenever he appeared on the scene and he made them, or more accurately allowed them, to glitter and shine. Yet in doing this he gave little of himself away. Perhaps he was like many people with normal personalities – there was nothing much to give away. So all those adjectives that we use to describe personality, such as 'stubborn', 'opinionated', 'angry', 'aggressive', 'anxious', 'miserable', 'misanthropic' and 'erratic', could never be applied to him. He could not be classified in any group or system. He never voted or gave an indication of his political opinions; merely by being what he was, he became a parody of himself. He was his own act, and there is nothing better in life to be praised and rewarded for just being what you are. Despite not having any conspicuous literary talent he is remembered by a plaque in Poet's Corner. The poem beneath could read:

> He was famous for being famous.
> He exposed – but did not blame us.

Personality difficulty

Definition: a long-standing, recurrent or intermittent disturbance in an individual's way of viewing the self, others and the world that is manifest in both emotional experience and expression, and in pat-

terns of behaviour. The disturbance is associated with some problems of social functioning and interpersonal relationships. However, impairment in functioning is not as severe as that found among people with formal personality disorder and is seen only in certain social and interpersonal contexts and may not be apparent elsewhere.

The Master of Gonville and Caius College at the time David Frost was an undergraduate was Sir James Chadwick. He discovered the neutron in 1932 and was awarded the Nobel Prize for Physics for this advance in 1935. He was heavily involved in the Manhattan Project that led to the development of the atomic bomb that was dropped on Hiroshima. As the key English member of this select group of scientists, he enabled successful joint collaboration with US colleagues and was rightly praised and honoured for his achievements.

So why bring up 'personality difficulty' in this context? Because James was a man who achieved an amazing amount but only after great struggle. He was liked greatly by his American colleagues because, unlike the more prominent Robert Oppenheimer (soon to be castigated in the McCarthy era), he was completely apolitical and detached from scheming or hidden agendas. He was noted by his Manhattan colleagues to have the interesting qualities of 'integrity, modesty, shyness and stiffness'. These were perfect qualities for a scientist in a laboratory with a passion for experiment, but not so ideal when dealing with people.

In 1948 James became Master of Gonville and Caius College, where he had been a fellow 20 years earlier. Being a Master of an Oxbridge college is like being head of a political party in which there are many factions all vying for influence, with many waiting and wanting to move either into your position or another one of power. The post requires managerial not scientific skills, and pragmatism has to be the order of the day. James tried to improve the scholastic status of the college by appointing the right people, but he failed to notice the undercurrents of ambition, envy and even spite that were swirling around him. Before long he was out-manoeuvred and resigned in despair, though not before a considerable amount of animosity had been created.

I was interviewed by him, if it can be called an interview, when I was seen as a schoolboy for a place at the college. This took place in the year before he resigned. The interview appeared to be carried out by the senior tutor, who asked all the standard questions but then became a little unstuck when he asked, 'What branch of medicine would you wish to pursue were you to be successful in coming here?' 'Psychiatry,' I answered promptly, relieved to be asked a question that required little thought. There was silence; the senior tutor was a language scholar. Suddenly, a voice from a figure on the sofa in the corner of the room broke the silence: 'What would you do with people; speed them up or slow them down?'

The voice came from James Chadwick, but I did not see his face as he was recumbent. 'I would be more likely to slow them down,' came the answer after a pause. It was all rather bizarre, but in retrospect I could imagine him looking up to the ceiling rather than facing a callow youth, and seeing the more predictable particles of the mini-solar systems of the atomic nucleus rather than the puzzle of a human shape with so many more imponderables.

James was a person with detached personality features. He was much happier in the laboratory with like-minded scientists than with the hurly-burly mixture of undergraduates and fellows in a Cambridge college. Being Master was prestigious, but it was not the right environment for him. So his detachment, showing itself with a limited ability to read people's motives and feelings, became a handicap and brought out personality difficulty, creating a degree of distress to others and to himself.

You might think that this is giving greater pathology to James than is justified, but it is not substantial pathology. I need to stress again that personality difficulty is not a mental disorder. As the definition states, it is only in certain situations that the problem is shown, and in James's case it may never have been made manifest at all if he had stayed in laboratory work until he retired.

Just how common is personality difficulty? It may surprise many, but our initial researches suggested more people have personality difficulty than any other grouping on the spectrum, including normal personality. In case this seems surprising, just recall again one of the characteristics, 'impairment in functioning is not as severe as that found among people with formal personality disorder and is seen only in certain social and interpersonal contexts and may not be apparent elsewhere'. If you think of your own circumstances there must have been times in certain situations when the ability to get on with others, your interpersonal function, is less than optimal. If you tend to have these difficulties whenever you encounter such situations then you have personality difficulty.

I have no problem putting myself in this group. I show a whole range of interpersonal difficulties when I am faced with petty administrators in my work. I know I should be more polite and careful in dealing with what appears to me utterly pointless obstruction, but instead I habitually lose my temper and say things I should not. So, not surprisingly, the administrator becomes even more obstructive and our interaction ends in a very bad way. Of course, I could just blame the system that allows such people to prosper or claim that I am the innocent party. But this is irrelevant. I behave badly and upset people, and this is enough to stamp 'personality difficulty' very clearly on my record.

Mild personality disorder

Definition: all individuals with mild personality disorder meet the essential requirements for personality disorder. They are able to maintain at least some relationships and occupational roles, as their

problems are discrete and only affect specific areas of personality func-
tioning. As a consequence, in some roles, their difficulties may not be
apparent. Mild personality disorder is not typically associated with
substantial harm to self or others.

Dora was a competent civil servant who became alcohol dependent. To be addicted to alcohol is not directly related to
personality, and everybody has the capacity to be alcohol dependent if they consume enough of our favourite poison. But
Dora had an additional problem: she was abnormally reliant on
others to maintain her self-esteem.

Unfortunately, despite being able to stop drinking on many
occasions, she returned to it again. The fact that she continued
drinking may not seem surprising to many, but in Dora's case
she returned to drinking because all her friends were drinkers
– and she could not really cope without them. It was the need
to feel accepted and to belong that brought her back time and
time again to the company that was to be her downfall. I was
aware of this excessive need for support as her therapist, as
she was so wedded to her appointments with me that she kept
them even after I had moved from London to Southampton
to take up a new post. What was frustrating was her ability to
escape alcohol dependence, to realize its dangers and yet return
to it again.

So the conversations we had tended to be a bit repetitive.

'So where are we today with the drinking?'
  'Well, I've had a pretty good two months really.'
  'Can you be more specific. Are you drinking now?'
  'Yes, just in the last two weeks.'
  'I see I am having to drag this out of you. What exactly has
  been going on?'
  'It's like this. As you know, I've had my early retirement
  confirmed and it's been a little bit tedious sitting at home
  sorting out all the papers I should have cleared up years ago. So
  I got a bit lonely and got in touch with Patrick [another drinker]
  again. He makes me feel better and gives me confidence.'

'And so you started back on the booze again?'

'Not intentionally. It's just when you meet people you like you drift into the pub and it just, as you know . . . develops.

'But you could still meet people in pubs and drink soft drinks or even water. You are not obliged to join in with the alcohol crowd.'

'You don't quite realize, Peter. These are the only people I feel at home with. Without them my life is one long tedious bore and I just feel on edge all the time. These are the only times when I feel I belong.'

Now, it is possible to conclude from this conversation that it is the alcohol talking, not the person. But I became convinced that the fundamental problem behind the drinking was that over the course of her life Dora had never been properly independent. She had relied on her family when growing up, right up to the time when she was married, and then relied on her husband until the marriage broke up, and then on her drinking friends subsequently. Without these supports she was anxious and miserable. Her personality problems were all in the negative affective domain.

Note that in mild personality disorder people 'are able to maintain at least some relationships and occupational roles, as their problems are discrete and only affect specific areas of personality functioning'. This was the reason why Dora was able to work effectively for 30 years until her drinking led to premature retirement, and why in many of her roles she appeared completely well.

Moderate personality disorder

Definition: all individuals with moderate personality disorder meet the essential requirements for personality disorder. Their problems are diffuse and affect several areas of personality functioning. As a consequence, social roles are markedly compromised, few friendships are maintained, normal work relationships are absent and conflict with others is persistent and common. Moderate personality disorder is often associated with a past history and future expectation of harm to self or others, but not to a degree that causes long-term damage or endangers life.

Malcolm was a teacher. He was not keen on receiving advice or help but I was asked to see him by his educational colleagues over his behaviour at school. He had been accused of bullying and several parents had objected, with comments that he selected pupils for personal criticism and often showed 'sadistic and grossly intolerant behaviour'. Further assessment, with both Malcolm and other colleagues, revealed that he ran his department as a personal fiefdom. He argued that he set very high standards and expected others to keep to them. Interviews with pupils showed that many were terrified of him, had nightmares in which they were ritually humiliated, and complained that there was nothing they could do to satisfy his high demands. Not known at the time of assessment, but reinforcing the conclusions made, was that at home Malcolm was equally dictatorial and treated his wife and children in the same way as his pupils.

The conversation about his pupils was difficult.

'There has been a series of complaints that you have been unnecessarily hard on certain pupils.'

'I am not surprised. If they do not meet our standards they will finish up as porters or post office workers. It is better that they notice this sooner rather than later.'

'But I am sorry to say that many parents do not agree with you. They claim that their sons and daughters are hard-working and want to succeed but you give them absolutely no encouragement. They claim that you "do everybody down" and never give any praise. You may know already of one boy who committed suicide recently, and his parents were convinced that he became depressed because of your behaviour.'

'This is absolute nonsense. The boy was not made of the right stuff. His parents are bound to complain because they want to avoid any responsibility for his death. My conscience is completely clear on this matter.'

'Do you not think, in view of these concerns, that you might

be able to change your behaviour and attitudes in some way?'
    'I will not tolerate being lectured to about my vocation.
I know I am a very good teacher, and my pupils – the ones I
know are good – achieve excellent results. I am not going to
prejudice their chances by mollycoddling [he stretched out this
word to emphasize his total opposition to any form of gentle
encouragement] boys and girls who are not up to scratch.'

Not surprisingly, the interview finished abruptly shortly afterwards. Because little changed in the subsequent 12 months,
Malcolm was dismissed from his position, but, because of his
good results with many of the pupils, this was reformulated as
early retirement.

So why do I regard Malcolm as having moderate personality
disorder? After all, at one level he was a successful teacher, even
though he let down some of his pupils quite badly. He was a
teacher at a time when the prevalent culture was one of control
and punishment for minor misdemeanours, well described by
Roald Dahl[2] when he was at a similar school:

> Four years is a long time to be in prison. It becomes twice as
> long when it is taken out of your life just when you are at your
> most bubbly best and the fields are all covered with daffodils
> and primroses . . . It seemed as if we were groping through
> an almost limitless black tunnel at the end of which there
> glimmered a small bright light, and if we ever reached it we
> would be 18 years old.

In Malcolm's case, his behaviour towards pupils at school,
often brutal and gratuitously demeaning, was replicated at
home, where he dominated his wife and family and made it
clear to all of them that his decisions were unchangeable and
should never be contradicted.

So I conclude that he had moderate personality disorder with
both obsessional (anankastic) and dissocial traits. One of the
major problems of people with this combination of characteristics is arrogance. He never seemed to conclude he might be

wrong and so never apologized. This is one of the problems with people as they get more personality disordered. They lack even a scintilla of mutual understanding and so cannot see how their behaviour could ever be construed as a problem. So even the suicide of one of the pupils – it was not the only one – did not lead to even a whisper of doubt or feelings that he should have acted differently.

Severe personality disorder

Definition: all individuals with severe personality disorder meet the essential requirements for personality disorder. Their problems in social interaction are profound and shown in multiple, and often all, aspects of personality functioning. Friendships are shallow or non-existent, occupational or vocational roles absent or severely compromised and societal responsibilities ignored. Severe personality disorder is usually associated with a past history and future expectation of severe harm to self or others that has caused long-term damage or has endangered life.

Sebastian was a difficult child who grew up to be a difficult man. He was very solitary at school with no real friends, but had talent in English and loved playing about with words, often tying them in polysyllabic knots and getting pleasure from untangling them afterwards. He became somewhat tiresome in his word playing and many conversations degenerated into arguments over lexicology that led up blind alleys. He was very disorganized in his personal life. It was something of a surprise to his family that he managed to get to university and somehow complete a degree in English. But this was the high spot. He was unable to work and ended up living at home with his mother.

He was stubborn and rigid, and at times became extremely angry with his mother when she tried to interfere with his lifestyle or tidy his room.

Sebastian became still more isolated as he got older, but developed a new trade. He became an eco-warrior. He decided that far too much was going to waste unnecessarily, so tables, chairs, out-of-date food, mattresses, half-empty pots of paint, plastic bags of every variety, old televisions and vacuum cleaners were all removed from tips and out of rubbish bins and stored in his flat. Not surprisingly, before long the living space in the flat became almost non-existent and Sebastian was confined to a tiny part of his living room, half a kitchen and a lavatory (the bath was filled up long ago). This behaviour now has a diagnostic label – hoarding disorder – and has attracted television producers and presenters as it has the propensity to create memorable images. Why people want to see rotting fruit, bevies of flies and furniture mountains that look at any moment as if they will topple beats me, but as I saw them every time I visited Sebastian at home, I must have become immune to their splendour.

Hoarding disorder did not replace Sebastian's personality disorder; it just reinforced it. He was visited less often and some of my colleagues would only enter his flat with masks or with pegs on their noses. He yearned to talk to people, even though his conversation consisted of long monologues with little chance of interjection, and his love of English grammar often led into lexicological cul-de-sacs from which there was no means of escape without causing offence.

Eventually the inevitable happened: television producers came to see him in the hope that they might be able to build a story around Sebastian's life that might hang together and appeal to viewers. I was less optimistic and concerned that a programme about him might just turn out to be a freak show – an unfortunate tendency to exaggerate mental symptoms and behaviour that is so extreme it stigmatizes rather than embraces mental illness.

The meeting was not a success. The two producers were women, smartly dressed in dark suits and mid-heel shoes, and they trod rather gingerly to the entrance to Sebastian's flat, always littered with bits of rubbish that had fallen off his latest acquisitions. I knocked on the door.

'Who is it?' called Sebasitan.

'Professor Tyrer. I'm with the two ladies from the television company that you agreed to see.'

'I'm on the lavatory.'

'OK, I appreciate this might not have been the best moment to call, but we can hang on a little longer.'

'You use the word "hang", Sebastian said, 'but what exactly are you going to hang on to while you are waiting?'

'I am just being colloquial here, Sebastian, but if you insist I will hang on to the door handle while we are waiting.'

''Why are you mocking me?'

'I am not mocking you, Sebastian,' I replied, 'just hoping you might get a move on as it is a little cold out here.'

There is silence. Five minutes later I ask, 'Sebastian, have you finished on the lavatory?'

'No.'

'Can I ask how long you are likely to be?'

'At least ten more minutes.'

'That is ridiculous, Sebastian. When I go to the lavatory everything is completed well within five minutes.'

'That explains why you are a professor of psychiatry and I am a poor miserable misfit.'

Within five minutes, Sebastian does indeed let us in, but because, in his mind, he has been hurried, he still has his pants down when he answers the door. My two companions try not to look shocked at the sight of a bearded, untrousered apparition looking like an audition for Caliban in Shakespeare's *The Tempest*, but fail miserably.

'Now, please pull your pants up, Sebastian. This is not very helpful behaviour.'

Sebastian sees a chance for more English lessons.

'If it is not helpful, it must be the opposite, unhelpful. Can you tell me, madam [turning to one of the producers], is it un-helpful to you that I have my pants down instead of up?'

The producer has gone green and is at the point of retching because of the smell coming from a display of rotting bananas on the table, so does not answer.

It is quite clear that we are not at the point of signing a contract for a programme, so I indicate that the interview is over. The two producers are at the door to the flat well before I am.

Sebastian, still with his pants down, asks, 'Why are you leaving now? We have only just started. Why have you rejected me again?'

'We have not rejected you,' I answer. 'It is just that this conversation has run its course.'

As we leave, Sebastian makes a play on 'course' and 'coarse' and is analysing coarse running as the door closes.

Shortly afterwards, Sebastian had to be admitted to hospital compulsorily as the flat had become a health hazard. We discussed the interview with the television producers later in hospital and the extent of his detachment from society was illustrated more clearly. He could not see any abnormality in his behaviour, did not think it was unreasonable to have his pants down, as he was going to return to the lavatory later (as we had interrupted him), and regarded us as completely unreasonable for leaving early. He was looking forward to seeing a television programme about him and our early departure added to his feelings of rejection.

The reasons why Sebastian has to be classified in the severe personality disorder category are his complete alienation from society, his aggression towards his mother, the potential public health hazards to those around him, and his absence of relationships apart from those with health professionals. He gives real flesh to the words in the definition 'friendships are shallow or non-existent, occupational or vocational roles absent or severely compromised, and societal responsibilities ignored'.

Despite this, all these problems, I and many others personally found him likeable and enjoyed our verbal jousting. He complained frequently about being 'the loneliest person in the world' and, despite all his absence of social skills, loved talking, often in a desperate monologue, as though dreading the time when the listener would leave and he would be returned to the isolated squalor of his flat.

The formal diagnosis for Sebastian is severe personality disorder with prominent traits in the anankastic, negative affective and detached domains. He also has hoarding disorder. You will note the tendency of people to attract many more domain traits when they have more severe personality disorders.

In the end, Sebastian was compelled to move into supervised care in a hostel. This is the fate of so many with severe personality disorder; some form of institutional care. This may be a hospital, a hostel, a supervised care home, a prison or another place of correction. This demonstrates the breakdown in societal bonds but almost invariably happens when there are no natural corrective forces to hold abnormal personality features at bay.

So here we have the full spectrum of personality displayed from normality to extreme severity. We are all on this spectrum, however much we may abhor it and claim that none of the examples bears any connection to our own personality. It requires both honesty and the ability to be confident in your skin in order to admit to some form of personality deviance. One of the messages of the new classification is that it cannot be stigmatizing to have a personality profile that is abnormal, because in statistical terms it is not abnormal at all if most people have some form of disturbance. I sometimes claim when lecturing that the people who ought to be stigmatized are those with normal personalities, those people whom you avoid in social situations because they always behave so well and are so boring! This usually leads to a titter of laughter because, of course, it seems quite ludicrous. But is it? I leave it for you to decide.

7

Borderline personality disorder

This condition is so important that it deserves a separate chapter. For many people, borderline personality disorder is the essence of personality abnormality, but it is not.

Its very name, borderline, gives the game away. It is a condition on the edge, overlapping with many others but not really belonging to any in the true sense. So although it has to have a central place in any book on personality disorder, the differences between it and virtually all other personality disorders need to be stressed right at the beginning. I should also declare my position. I do not think that borderline personality disorder should be included among the other personality disorders; it is better described as an emotional dysregulation syndrome.

Imagine a perfectly normal person who has strong desires and feelings, but who cannot predict them in any coherent way. Each emotion seems to have a life of its own, rampaging independently and chaotically through daily life and leaving havoc in its wake. Now you have a sense of the core of the borderline condition. The combination of sober intentions and mad emotions is an awful mixture, and is best, and most ably, described by people with the condition:

> 'Being a borderline feels like eternal hell. Nothing less. Pain, anger, confusion, never knowing how I'm gonna feel from one minute to the next. Hurting because I hurt those whom I love. Feeling misunderstood. Nothing gives me pleasure.'

> 'Separation anxiety, fear of abandonment, self-harm and emotional instability prevented me from experiencing what

should have been the typical life of a teenager. I spent my days in isolation, not understanding the overwhelming emotions that attacked me from every side, often crying myself to sleep wondering why the feelings just wouldn't go away, and why I couldn't put a name to them.'

'I knew that depression didn't explain some of my symptoms. I had too much going on for that to be true. The symptoms can include eating problems, impulsiveness, self-harm, mild psychosis, and hectic, unstable relationships. All of these I experience at least three times a week.'

'Throughout my teens I failed to develop an identity, falling behind academically, socially and emotionally. It felt like I had got "stuck" at age 11 when the problems began and that my body and mind were developing but my sense of self and capacity to regulate emotion lagged way behind. It wasn't until I was finally diagnosed with borderline personality disorder that I began to realise what all these symptoms meant, and I was finally able to start unpicking my past in order to understand my present.' (Mental Health Foundation's website, 'Kayla's story: Living with borderline personality disorder')

There are dozens of similar stories that could be told by those with borderline personality disorder, all of which demonstrate the same features of emotions galloping completely out of control. Yet this is quite different from the other moods of depression, anxiety and anger, which may be highly unpleasant but at least fit in, or are usually described as congruent, with other aspects of behaviour.

When people are what psychiatrists describe as *clinically* depressed or anxious, or both, they at least have time to adjust or, at least, compensate for their feelings. Anxious people avoid anxiety-provoking situations, depressed people tend to isolate themselves from others, and often can disguise how they really feel by rehearsing or planning their interactions with other people. But when these moods arise suddenly, not only without warning, but often at times when there is important personal interaction that requires reflection, they throw a massive spanner into the complex pattern of relationships that can be immensely damaging.

So how has all this become tied up with the notion of personality disorder? Let us answer this by first looking at the current ways of describing borderline personality disorder in both the American (DSM) and international (ICD) systems. In summary, they describe:

1 fears of being abandoned;
2 unstable and often intense interpersonal relationships;
3 uncertainty over identity;
4 a tendency to act on impulse at times of high emotion;
5 recurrent self-harm;
6 instability of emotions that can be triggered by external or internal factors;
7 feelings of internal emptiness;
8 displays of temper or anger;
9 brief episodes of dissociation or psychotic symptoms.

Although all these are all included as features of a personality disorder, if you consider that the inability to control your emotions is the central element of all of them, they fall into place. If you do not know who you fundamentally are as a person you can doubt your identity and become detached or dissociated, and sudden unexpected emotions can show themselves as anger, emptiness, irritability, suicidal behaviour and impulsiveness. In between these emotional explosions you can behave perfectly normally but can also appreciate how terrible your (often very recent) behaviour has been, and this explains the tremendous guilt and soul-searching that can follow.

Marsha Linehan, the single-minded psychologist who, partly through her own experience of emotional dysregulation, developed dialectical behaviour therapy, the best known of treatments for borderline personality disorder, has always considered the condition to be primarily a disorder of emotional regulation. She describes it as pervasive 'when the ability to regulate emotions occurs across a wide range of emotions, adaptation problems and situational contexts'.[1] The condition became absorbed into the group of personality disorders for two reasons: because the clinicians who treated it were working mainly in the field of personality, and because there was a formal split in diagnosis in the USA in 1980, when psychiatric disorders were separated into mental disorders (Axis I of the classification) or personality disorders (Axis II). Borderline hovered on the brink at first, as, being borderline, it always does, and then toppled into the personality disorder Axis II group, and has been there ever since.

Some people with the condition are pleased with the diagnosis of borderline personality disorder. This is not because they like the name, but because they realize that the description of the condition exactly matches their own experience. As Kayla said, 'It wasn't until I was finally diagnosed with borderline personality disorder that I began to realize what all these symptoms meant, and I was finally able to start unpicking my past in order to understand my present.'

But some people find this label deeply unattractive:

When it dawned on me that 'having a histrionic flavour to her presentation' did not describe the packet of crisps I was holding, but my dress sense!
Well, I was understandably indignant.
Now it just amuses me
To trawl through the list of character traits
That define me to be an aberration

Who actually believes this diagnosis
To be anything more than judgemental hocus pocus.[2]

If we now compare borderline personality disorder with the other personality disorders, these distinctions become even more prominent.

The distinctiveness of borderline personality disorder

1 People with borderline personality disorder feel terrible about their symptoms and do everything possible to get rid of them.

This may not look very different from all other mental disorders but what is called 'treatment-seeking behaviour' is far from common in those with other personality problems. Although people with other personality disorders have many problems in their relationships with others, they do not usually want to change their personalities.[3] They often blame others for the difficulties they create, and so justify their behaviour. Any suggestion that they should seek help for their personality problems is quickly dismissed. This also explains why so few of them present with their personality problems in the form of complaints, even though they can be teased out quite easily.

This is not true of those who have borderline personality disorder. They know only too well how much their feelings and behaviour are distressing others, but cannot stop repeating them, commonly with intense regret afterwards for the trouble they have caused. In this respect, borderline personality disorder behaves like an Axis I disorder, not an Axis II one.

2 People with borderline personality disorder have fluctuating, not consistent, behaviour.

One of the central elements of the definition of personality disorder is an abnormal behaviour pattern that is 'pervasive and clearly maladaptive to a broad range of personal and social situations'. This applies to people with borderline personality disorder for some of the time, but at other times, if things go right, they can be outstanding and stimulating companions with no hint of interpersonal conflict. However, once the emotional rollercoaster is generated, everything can descend into chaos. This other personality could not be further removed from those such as the meticulous, hyperconscientious, rigid personality of the obsessional person. It used to be said that the famous German philosopher Emanuel Kant was so ordered in his daily life that he took the same walk through Koenigsberg, his home town in Prussia, at precisely 4 o'clock in the afternoon, and that his neighbours used to check their clocks and watches when they saw him because his timing was so accurate. This could not be further removed from the person with borderline personality disorder, who may have already smashed his or her watch in anger in an argument well before 4 p.m.

It is also not hard to see that people with borderline personality disorder are much more distressed than those of other personality types as life is so unpredictable and upsetting for them.

3 The features of borderline personality disorder are all related to emotions, not ingrained personality patterns.

It has been noted already that the features of borderline personality disorder are primarily related to emotional dysregulation. When personality patterns are persistent and predictable, they are commonly described as 'traits', or habitual patterns of thought, behaviour and emotion. Although emotion comes into this definition, the emotions of borderline personality disorder are not habitual, repetitive and constant. The emotions and behaviour of someone with borderline personality disorder represent a dizzying rollercoaster that never stays still, threatens to toss the occupants off at every major turn, and is completely unpredictable in its course.

4 Most personality disorders had some advantages in our evolutionary past; borderline personality disorder has none.

Although we regard the features of personality disorder as counterproductive in modern society it was not always so. The antisocial hunter gatherers of the past were aggressive in battle and highly successful warriors. They were also highly respected, although this respect was often tinged with fear. Similarly, the highly anxious and dependent mother in the tribe would be subservient to the men around her, but also very careful to look after her children in a very dangerous world. The obsessional cave dweller who made sure that the entrances were well hidden and defended, and any watercourses diverted so that the cave would not be flooded, also was a great help in ancient societies. This offers an important clue to treatment, which we shall come across later. The environment of these societies was completely different from those currently in our overcrowded planet, and different patterns of behaviour were needed for them.

It is just not possible to see any advantages in evolutionary terms for borderline personality disorder. At no time in the history of the human race have the features of borderline personality disorder shown any possible gain. It again puts the borderline condition into the group of mental disorders, all of which create some level of biological disadvantage.

Is borderline personality disorder wrongly classified as a personality disorder?

The answer to this question is yet again, borderline. Although the emotional dysregulation underpinning the disorder is better thought of as a mental illness (where it would probably be included among other mood disorders such as anxiety and depression), it is so extensive in its presentation that it disrupts personality function too. When I and my research colleagues have looked at the way in which people with borderline personality disorder group together in terms of the domain traits described in Chapter 5, we find they are literally all over the place. As you might guess, the domain of 'negative affectivity' is very prominent, but so is the disinhibited (impulsive) domain, as well as the dissocial (antisocial) one in many people. But, as already noted, these are not persistent personality traits, but yo-yo gremlins that come and go at different times.

Treatment differences

The treatment of borderline personality disorder is very different from that of any other personality disorder.

Because borderline personality disorder is such an unpleasant condition that is seen as such by those who experience it, help is often demanded, frequently as an emergency. The most common form of emergency assistance is the treatment of suicidal behaviour. There are many reasons for suicidal thinking and behaviour and they extend far beyond the field of personality, but it is the problem of self-harm above all else that has led to so much attention being given to this condition in clinical practice.

One in ten of all people who harm themselves commit suicide eventually, and so self-harm should never be considered as trivial. One of the reasons why those with borderline personality disorder are unfairly criticized is a perceived impression that much of the self-harm carried out by people with this condition is unnecessary and allegedly carried out only to attract attention. This is almost always untrue but is a natural consequence of a condition in which emotions can fluctuate so greatly in a brief period of time that people can appear completely well shortly after intense emotional anguish. So these people seem completely different from those with severe depression or psychosis in which the features of the illness are only too apparent at the time of presentation.

Because people with borderline personality disorder are the ones who either seek treatment or present for treatment in emergencies, by far the largest number of effective treatments for personality disorder are found in the borderline condition. They are all described in Table 1, but also come into the management of other personality disorders as there is so much overlap between them.

When you look at Table 1, it is impressive, but when it comes to deciding which treatment is the best, it is impossible to judge

Table 1 Psychological treatment for borderline personality disorder

Name of treatment	Main proponents	Central feature	Evidence of benefit
Mentalization-based treatment (MBT)	Anthony Bateman and Peter Fonagy	Mentalization (mutual understanding of feelings and behaviour)	Seems to work
Dialectical behaviour therapy (DBT)	Marsha Linehan	Skills training and mindfulness	Seems to work
Transference-focused therapy (TFT)	Otto Kernberg	Self-understanding in relationships	Seems to work
Schema-focused therapy (SFT)	Jeffrey Young	Changing maladaptive patterns of feelings and behaviour	Seems to work
Cognitive behaviour therapy (CBT)	Aaron (Tim) Beck	Collaborative restructuring of unhelpful beliefs	Seems to work
Cognitive analytic therapy (CAT)	Anthony Ryle	Combined CBT and analytic approaches	Seems to work
Systems training for emotional predictability and problem solving (STEPPS)	Nancie Blum	Combined problem-solving and skills-based educational package	Seems to work
Acceptance and commitment, therapy (ACT)	Robert Zettle	Structured acceptance and mindfulness	Seems to work
Structured clinical management (SCM)	Anthony Bateman and Roy Krawitz	An amalgam of the central elements of all the above	Seems to work

them adequately. Like the Caucus Race in Lewis Carroll's *Alice's Adventures in Wonderland*, each therapy can start and stop when it chooses and, in the end, everybody wins and gets a prize.

There is something wrong here, however. When you have a new psychological therapy appearing for borderline personality disorder almost annually, and when each of them seems to have a magic ingredient that defines its key element, why is it that they all seem to have equal effectiveness? There are two issues competing here. Each treatment has a guru (sometimes two) whose statements represent the essence of the therapy. For someone suffering the chaos of borderline symptom, these pronouncements are like manna from heaven: 'This therapy has the answer and I must seek out its truth.'

In the longer run, after many months of different types of group and individual therapy, these approaches have fairly limited gains. They all appear to reduce the incidence of self-harm, with DBT possibly doing so a little more than others, but the jury is still out on this matter too. This is a very important outcome, but these therapies do not have nearly as much of an effect on general functioning and well-being, so people lose many of the characteristics of borderline personality disorder, yet are not happy people.

Anthony Bateman and Roy Krawitz[4] have helped greatly to puncture some of the more grandiose claims of individual treatments by amalgamating their essential elements into 'structured clinical management' (SCM). This approach has been shown to be just as good as the other apparently more specialized treatments and combines supportive and consistent care, anticipation and planning of crisis situations, medication monitoring and assertive follow-up if appointments are missed. (This last element is particularly important as so many people with borderline problems break off contact with their therapists and then regret it later.)

I also feel that the messy classification of personality disorder is largely responsible for this unsatisfactory state of affairs. The borderline pot stirs together many different conditions (technically it is a heterogeneous diagnosis) that should and could be separated in a way that allows tailor-made treatments to be developed. Is it too much to hope that the new classification of personality disorder might help this process on its way?

This account should not be too gloomy to a reader who has, or knows someone with, borderline personality disorder. Because it is such a potpourri of a diagnosis, it includes some people who respond very well to therapy, even if it is sometimes prolonged. For those who feel despairing of improvement, I suggest you read Barbara Taylor's heart-wrenching but eventually heart-warming book about her own experiences and the saintly psychoanalyst who never gave up seeing her and who stayed the full course.[5]

Dissociation

There is another element to the borderline phenomenon that adds to its complexity. When stresses become intolerable to the psyche it has to escape somehow and it can do this, quite successfully, by dissociation. You will note this in the ninth operational criterion for personality disorder – 'transient stress-related paranoid ideation or severe dissociated symptoms' (see p. 85). Dissociation is often known as splitting. If you are able to split off highly unpleasant emotions by, in effect, forgetting you have them, you have a solution, however temporary, to your problem.

Here is one personal example.

Lily (not her real name) was in hospital with a diagnosis of personality disorder. She appeared to be getting better and so I thought it might help her, and the clinical team looking after her, to ask her to explain what it was like to have the symptoms of emotional dysregulation to some medical students who were attached to the team. She consented to this readily and appeared to enjoy the question-and-answer session with the students, who thanked her profusely after the session.

But it was a mistake to involve her in this teaching experience. Four hours later I received an urgent phone call from the police at a town 150 miles away.

'Do you happen to know someone called Lily X?'

'Yes, she is at present a patient in our hospital.'

'No, she isn't. She's in the police station here. We've just had to lift her off the railway line outside the station – before the next express train came through.'

It took him some time to convince me that his Lily was the same as mine but clearly this was the case and an ambulance transported her back to hospital in London. It so happened that our hospital was being visited the following day by Marsha Linehan, the inventor of dialectical behaviour therapy. As I was getting rather out of my depth, I asked if she might see Lily with me. We walked into the interview room together.

For those who have not met Marsha Linehan here is a pen portrait; it helps to understand what followed. Marsha has presence, and by this I mean that when she walks into a room, usually in clothes that seem to sweep all in front of her like a magisterial carpet cleaner, everyone stops what they are doing and looks at her in anticipation of something important happening.

So I felt a little intimidated as I accompanied her to see Lily. 'Hi,' Marsha said to her, 'so what has been going on?' I was quickly lost in a highly charged rip-rap exchange of conversation in which phrases like 'on autopilot', 'no control' and 'just a spectator' occurred frequently.

'Absolutely classical dissociation,' said Marsha to me afterwards. Lily had been stressed by the meeting with the medical students and it had reopened wounds of the past. She had reacted by leaving the hospital and getting a one-way ticket to the Midlands, getting off the train at the right station, walking up the platform, leaving it where it slopes to the ground and then lying across the tracks. This seemed like a planned suicide attempt, but Lily insisted it was not. 'It wasn't me who got that ticket, went on that journey and laid down on those rails. It was someone else. I was on autopilot and could not do anything about it. It just had to happen.'

Dissociative identity disorder, or multiple personality disorder, is the extreme form of dissociation. This is when the whole personality dissociates and two or more, often many more, distinct personalities emerge. These are often contradictory, opposing personalities, described most evocatively by Robert Louis Stevenson in his book *The Strange Case of Dr Jekyll and Mr Hyde*. So whereas Dr Jekyll is upright, proper, kind, supportive and gentle, his alter ego, Mr Hyde, is violent, sadistic, antisocial and, quite simply, terrifying. But are they different parts of the same person or different people? That is one of the conundrums of the subject.

Here am I, arguing all the way through this book, that personality is relatively constant, no matter how much on the surface may change, yet here we have a condition where the whole personality – traits, dispositions, behaviours, the whole caboodle – can shift into an entirely new dimension. How can this happen?

Part of this can be explained by trauma. Many of those with dissociative personality disorder, as well as borderline disorder, have experienced major trauma, sexual and physical, as children, and this is a time when personality is developing and is most vulnerable to disruption. When faced with intolerable stresses and with no obvious hope of succour, the developing personality structure can just opt out. 'I can't cope with this awfulness, I am just going to park it somewhere else.'

The existing developing personality continues as before, almost assuming that nothing has happened, and on the surface appears to be maturing normally. But it is not. It has only survived by the other personality, or personalities, brooding in its car park waiting to be activated. This other personality often has some of the attributes of the actors, if we can call them such, in the abusive situation. The quiet sufferer, the aggressive sadist, the truculent adolescent, the passive baby, can all be represented in the alters (other personalities) and can be activated by dissociation at different times. The original abuser had power and this is reflected frequently in at least one of the alters, mimicking some of this behaviour. In classical dissociation, as originally defined, there is total amnesia (forgetfulness) of the personalities, and when the split only occurs infrequently the person may assume a completely different lifestyle, move to a different part of the country and take up a different occupation.

Dissociative identity disorder is said to be quite common, affecting about 1 per cent of the population. But there are varying degrees of dissociation, with many people being able to engage with their alters when apparently needed, and not having complete amnesia when they change over their personalities. There are also some who could be said to bring the diagnosis into disrepute, by alleging dissociation at times when it was not true, but could be of inestimable value if they could persuade people that they had dissociated into different personalities.

One of the most famous cases was that of Thomas Huskey. This took place in Knoxville, Tennessee in 1999, but dragged on for many years afterwards.

After four women were killed, three of them prostitutes, Huskey was charged with their murders. Huskey recorded a tape in which he confessed to the murders. At this point everything seemed very simple. But two defence lawyers construed an unusual defence. They argued that the confession on the tape was not Huskey at all. Even though Huskey was speaking, the voice was completely different, that of a completely different personality named 'Kyle'. Other personalities were also found, following further interrogation by the defence, but Kyle was the actual killer.

The legal system has tied itself in knots over this issue ever since. According to Tennessee law, not substantially different from English law, if Huskey was mentally ill, he would not be

> responsible for criminal conduct, if at the time of such conduct, as a result of a mental disease or defect, he lacks substantial capacity either to appreciate the wrongfulness of his conduct or to conform his conduct to the requirements of the law.

The prosecution argued that Huskey was a psychopath who had made up his additional personalities as a way of avoiding responsibility for his actions. One of the doctors called by the prosecution, Dr Herbert Spiegel, voiced the view of many in describing Huskey as a man with 'an incredible ability to ma-nipulate people. He is now, if anything, manipulating the whole state of Tennessee.' Not surprisingly, the jury were completely split on the case, half arguing that he was mentally ill (that is, he had dissociative identity disorder) at the time of the killings (just like Hyde in Stevenson's novel) and the other half concluding he was a phony who had manufactured the whole story.

Borderline and (true) dissociative identity disorder have a lot in common. There are dissociative elements in much of the behaviour of people who have borderline symptoms. Comments such as, 'I couldn't believe I was doing this', 'I was behaving like someone in a film', 'I just got taken over by my emotions' are not true dissociation but illustrate the alien nature of much of the actions of the borderline person. This helps to explain why I think borderline personality disorder is so different from other personality disorders, and may ultimately be thought of as more of a dissociative one.

After reading about all the unusual features of borderline personality disorder that make it so different from the rest of personality disturbance it is reasonable for all to ask the question, 'Is this condition an abnormality of personality or something very different?' My view, already expressed above, is that it is primarily a disturbance of emotional regulation, and by using the word 'regulation' I am separating the condition from other emotional disorders such as anxiety and depression where the symptoms are more predictable. And because all the disturbed emotions are so scattered around the psyche in the borderline person, like gunshot holes in a fabric waiting to be torn, they impact on personality and functioning to a much greater extent than in other emotional disorders, so it is hardly surprising that personality function is disturbed.

This is not just academic nit-picking. If we are to get a proper understanding of what it is to be borderline we cannot leave it, as its name suggests, on the edge of mental illness. It belongs, but where? The latest research on the human genome suggests it belongs to the group of serious mental illnesses such as bipolar disorder and schizophrenia, but this notion has a long way to go before it can be verified. So where are we at present? In true borderline tradition this important condition has been left precariously adrift in the new international classification of personality disorders. It is with the other personality disorders, but it is not. Balancing on a tight rope separated from the main classification is a 'borderline specifier'. The clinician classifies according to severity but does not need to go any further. Borderline will do. But, in the long term, it will not.

8

Taming personality disorder

Now we come to the reckoning. Do you, or someone close to you, have some sort of personality disturbance? If so, what can be done about it? As you might guess, the answer to the first part of this question is unlikely to be negative. What almost everybody finds is that it is much easier finding personality disturbance in others rather than in oneself. This is not surprising, as we tend to protect ourselves from the harshest of criticisms unless we have a personality structure prone to self-flagellation. This is unfortunately true of the borderline syndrome discussed earlier.

So it is worthwhile trying to be as objective as possible in assessing personality and it is useful to break this down into elements that are relatively neutral. The following procedure can be used with anyone you know – let us just label this person X.

- Does X usually have harmonious relationships with other people?
- Are there any people or groups of people whom X persistently avoids or creates trouble with?

If the first answer is 'yes' and the second 'no', then check again to be absolutely certain they are not telling fibs. If they are not, they can probably be placed in the small group called 'no personality disturbance'. Some people might call them 'nice but boring', but these critics might be a little envious.

Many more people would come into the 'avoid or create trouble category', even though most of their relationships are harmonious. For this group we have further questions.

1 Do you avoid these people because they upset or irritate you in any way?
2 When you cannot avoid them, do you feel uncomfortable or distressed in their presence? Do you find it difficult to understand these people and how they function in life?

This is the area of personality difficulty, and if the answers to any of these questions is 'yes', I suspect you (or X) have a degree of personality difficulty. Why do I come to this conclusion? Can't we all have likes and dislikes without being labelled as abnormal in some way? Well, we have to keep a sense of proportion. As a football supporter it may be perfectly reasonable to avoid groups of supporters of an opposing club, but this is not always true and hardly a persistent problem. Here I am discussing groups that you might be expected to meet and mix with, either at work or in your spare time, yet cannot abide their company.

The most frequent response to this situation is to blame this group rather than yourself: 'I don't mix with them because they don't like me, and anyway I have nothing in common with them.' This may be partly true, but you contribute to this as well. In the first chapter of this book I admitted that I had personality difficulty. I avoid groups or people who stimulate my anti-authority feelings, not least as I feel I might be provoked into saying something I shouldn't if I remained in their company. When I was 14 and queueing up to go into a cinema (you needed to queue up in those days), we saw a man being chased by a policeman. I remember my father saying, 'I wonder if we should be giving some help,' to be contradicted promptly by my Irish mother, 'What do you mean? We should trip the copper up.' My own feelings at the time chimed with my mother's, even though I could not possibly support these views if asked in the cold light of day.

So if you avoid situations where you might do things you regret, or if you do enter them and get into trouble, the easy option of blaming others is not good enough, particularly if the problem keeps repeating.

It has taken quite a few chapters to describe all the features of personality dysfunction – and by dysfunction we include everybody who does not fall into the small area of 'normal personality'. So I am assuming that most of my readers are interested to know where they, and others close to them, are on the personality spectrum, but before we evaluate this, we need to be sure that many of the misconceptions about personality disorder are no longer in our minds. Here they are.

1 Although we still have to use the term 'personality disorder', there is no clear distinction between those who have a disorder and those who do not.
2 Although personality is relatively fixed and only changes gradually over time, personality dysfunction changes a great deal depending on circumstances and environmental factors.
3 Most people with personality dysfunction do not want to change their personalities and so abhor the prospect of 'treatment', no matter what others might wish.
4 Adjectival descriptions of personality such as 'narcissistic', 'histrionic', 'dependent', 'schizoid' and 'passive-aggressive' are now redundant.
5 Borderline personality disorder is a highly unusual condition that overlaps with other personality disorders, but is primarily a persistent problem of emotional regulation.
6 A large proportion of people with other mental disorders also have personality dysfunction, but this is often not recognized.
7 The problems in interpersonal functioning that are central to personality disturbance are often blamed on other people rather than on their originator.
8 There is absolutely no reason why those with personality dysfunctions should be stigmatized as most people have

some degree of this dysfunction, even though this cannot be described as personality disorder.

One of the reasons why I analysed my own personality in the first chapter of this book is that I wanted to do, consciously for the first time and over a long timescale, what I am asking the reader to do now. Before we examine the personalities of those about us we should look carefully at our own, even though it may be uncomfortable. It is curious how attractive it is to look at errors in others but not those in ourselves.

As interpersonal functioning is at the core of personality disorder, it is worthwhile looking at all the occasions in the past where you had problems in interacting with other people. There are few people who have not had any obvious difficulties in this respect. Some are genuinely saint-like, always seeing the best in people and defusing every hint of conflict. But most of us get annoyed, behave badly, irritate others, have periods when we avoid or will not speak to some people, or say and do things that we regret afterwards.

If these experiences are true of you it does not mean you have any personality problems, but if they have occurred repeatedly it is quite another matter. And, when they do recur, there is a natural tendency to blame the other person for the problems rather than yourself. The opposite may occur, when you blame yourself unduly and unfairly, but this is much less common. There are also others, particularly those in the borderline category, who oscillate wildly between blaming others and then blaming themselves.

Assuming you have some degree of personality dysfunction, the next stage is to decide its level of severity. Personality difficulty is by far the biggest group here. This level applies to people who have repeated problems in some situations but not others. Here we are talking about normal situations that tend to recur in people's lives, not ones that are highly unusual. So if you only have real difficulties in relating to people when you are being interviewed for a very important job, this is a specific social anxiety that is not directly related to personality. But if you lose your cool when being interviewed for any task, and if this occurs repeatedly, this could come under the heading of 'problems with authority figures', and be personality difficulty.

People with personality difficulty often show no evidence of any problems away from these aggravating settings. It is sometimes quite easy to pick up those who have personality difficulty from ordinary conversations. If you happen to meet a person only in one situation – say, for example, on a train on the way to work – all your experience will be based on this one environment. So if the other person seems to be uneasy and unduly sensitive because they are bothered about other people overhearing your conversation, you can be left with the idea that they are normally suspicious or difficult people. Later, when you talk to someone else who knows that person well you realize that it is just the situation that has created the problem.

Why do I not use the word 'treating' here, and why is it not mentioned in the title of this book? The reason is that I am trying to be accurate about the degree to which we can effect change in people with personality disorder, and, as we have found, for most people with personality dysfunction treatment is the last thing that is wanted. About 85 per cent of people with personality disorder do not want to be treated.[1] They regard their personalities as an integral part of their nature and do not want to have them altered. This does not mean that their problems have gone unnoticed – they are often all too prominent – but it is very common for others to be regarded as the source of any problems that may arise. So when it comes to dealing with this large number of people (probably around 20 million in the UK) there is no question of providing treatment. The answer is to minimize the impact of the personality problems so ideally they create no disturbance. If this sounds a little odd it is not meant to be. What we must always realize about personality disorder is that it involves other people, and if those people can make adjustments in the appropriate way the elements of disorder lessen or simply disappear.

What about the 15 per cent of people who have personality disorder and want, sometimes desperately, to be treated? Most of these have 'borderline personality disorder', which, as we noted in the previous chapter, is being allowed into the new classification even though it does not properly belong there.

But we cannot remove borderline from the personality spectrum even though it is so unusual. Hagop Akiskal, an expert on mood disorders, mocks the diagnosis of borderline as 'an adjective in search of a noun'.[2] I sometimes think it should be a verb. 'To borderline' would describe behaviour that is disruptive, confrontational and impulsive. 'There you go again, stop borderlining' might be a better form of defusion than the more common direct reactions.

In the new classification there is an option for the diagnosis of borderline personality disorder, but this is only exercised when the severity level – mild, moderate or severe personality disorder – has been decided. Most of those with the more severe form of the disorder would probably have 'domain traits' in the negative affective, dissocial and/or disinhibited groups. By removing the diagnosis of 'borderline' from the description 'personality disorder' we are not denying the existence of the many people who suffer enormously because of the unpredictability of their emotional states and all the troubles that these bring in tandem. We also hope that the new classification will enable the treatments that currently exist, and that are described in more detail below, to be better focused. About one in six more people with personality disorder currently seem to be in the borderline group, and this accounts for nearly 1 in 100 of the population. Nobody is suggesting that all of these should require intensive treatment; the new classification should help enormously in making the choice.

You will notice that the word 'treatment' is now beginning to creep into the text. This is because, despite its position on the fringes of personality disorder, borderline has attracted the most interest in terms of interventions. This is hardly surprising as this is the condition par excellence in which people are desperately seeking relief from highly unpleasant symptoms and behaviour. Because there is such a demand for treatment, and a supply of therapists who are all desperately keen to improve the lot of people who are clearly suffering so badly, any positive results have a tendency to be greatly overstated.

How many people have personality difficulty?

The new classification has not yet been used widely, so the figures can only be estimates, but here they are:

- no personality dysfunction – 35 per cent
- personality difficulty – 48 per cent
- mild personality disorder – 12 per cent
- moderate personality disorder – 4.5 per cent
- severe personality disorder – 0.5 per cent.

These figures may come as a shock, but are extrapolated, together with other data, from a recent study of the UK population.[3] How can it be that most of the population have some degree of personality disturbance? Is this not another example of the medicalization of minor degrees of mental suffering that do not deserve any label? These are fair questions, but I will answer them with an example.

At the time of writing, I have just come back from visiting a hospital. It has not been used as such for many years, but the maternity ward still looks clean and clinical, with a stone floor, shining walls and impeccable hygiene. The nurses there were well trained and committed to their work and many mothers delivered their babies successfully there, with all the staff showing great competence and professionalism. The only thing that differentiated this hospital from other similar units was that, after the birth of each baby, despite the efforts to ensure a safe and healthy birth, both the mother and infant were murdered by injections of phenol. Yes, you can read that sentence again; it is quite shocking.

This maternity unit was in Birkenau, part of the Auschwitz-Birkenau extermination camp run by the German Nazi SS in Poland between 1940 and 1945. Most of the nurses there came from middle-class families. At the time of recruitment, a post in the civilian part of the SS was considered to be a step up in society – the pay was good and there were reliable prospects of promotion. Yet these nurses, all of them, carried out these murders daily in the belief that, by removing Jews, Poles and gypsies from the world, they were performing a service to humanity.

Personality difficulty is characterized by being demonstrated in only certain settings. Auschwitz-Birkenau was a very unusual setting, but the fact that many health professionals there had good relationships and apparently normal and satisfying lives away from their workplace shows that most of them could not be described as evil, sadistic or in any way grossly abnormal in their behaviour. But inside the maternity unit (and elsewhere in the camp), everything changed. The rules of normal behaviour were suspended. Sadism ruled.

This extreme example shows the tremendous impact that the environment can have on our behaviour. When I suggest that personality difficulty is extremely common as well as creating problems in life (and there is evidence that it does), I am particularly referring to often brief, but recurring, episodes when people are placed in environments in which they feel uncomfortable or profoundly detest, and react accordingly – badly. Several examples have been mentioned already but there are dozens more. Places in which assessments and interviews are made, public meetings, working with others in restricted space, formal ceremonies, summer camps, crowd occasions, musical evenings, bingo halls, communal dinners, lecture halls, leisure clubs – at least one of these is likely to make you cringe and avoid whenever you can. All of them involve interaction with other people. Personality disorder, unlike any other mental condition, cannot occur in isolation. You cannot have a personality disorder if you are alone on a desert island.

Many more problems arise in people with personality difficulty if there seems to be no way of avoiding the situations that provoke the difficult behaviour. If you are forced to work in a setting that is anathema to you but cannot see an easy way of changing it, then explosions are just round the corner. Sometimes people do not realize they and the situation are reacting together so badly and only blame themselves or others for creating the trouble. This is when some assistance, such as nidotherapy (discussed in the next chapter), may be indicated. When stuck in a rut it is difficult to see out.

But we also need to remember that personality difficulty is not a formal diagnosis in the new classification of personality disorder. It is part of the spectrum that, somewhat artificially, crosses the line into personality disorder at the next stage. I like to think that having a personality difficulty makes you a more interesting person – but I may be biased.

For people with mild personality disorder, whose personality problems are not situational, there are several options. One of these may include seeking medical advice, preferably from a doctor or other health professional who knows you well, sadly becoming rarer than it used to be, and much of the advice given is likely to be along the lines of nidotherapy or other environmental change. One of the main stumbling blocks for people with mild personality disorder is the refusal to admit there is anything wrong, so that everything is blamed on others. This is where improved mutual understanding comes in. If you are able to appreciate, even at a relatively low level of detection, that the negative way other people react to you could at least be partly explained by how you appear to them, you are making progress. So people who chatter incessantly and complain about everything under the sun, yet cannot understand why their company is avoided or those who are persistently irritable and angry and find fault with others, may have to be gently reminded, or better still remind themselves, that they could be a cause, not a consequence, of others' difficulties.

So what about treatment? Is personality disorder, taken in general, treatable? The simple answer is no. But that does not mean it cannot be helped or reduced to a level that is of little concern. It is a condition that is like the blood disorder haemophilia, in which the normal ability of the blood to clot is absent. This disease cannot be reversed, but by regular injections of a clotting agent it can be managed very successfully.

There are some important differences between personality disturbance and haemophilia. Nobody, unless for extreme religious reasons, refuses treatment for haemophilia, but most people with personality disorder would refuse to have treatment even if it was offered. This may seem hard to believe, but personality is the essential part of 'I am', and does not want to be changed into 'I was'. So even though personality disorder can bring a host of troubles in its wake, the thought of having your very nature altered is just a no-go. Second, we have no predictable, instant treatments, even temporary ones, for personality disorder in the same way that we have for haemophilia. If we had, we could use them for a short time to become the people others would like us to be, before returning to the familiar ungracious and crotchety creatures that are comfortable in their own skins, even if they are detested by others.

Some people maintain that is far too gloomy a view and insist that we now have a large number of highly effective treatments for personality disorder that are revolutionizing attitudes to the subject. This opinion is held by some who work very hard, and with great skill, particularly in treating borderline personality disorder, many of whom devote their professional lives to the different treatments described in the previous chapter. But if we cast a cold eye on all these treatments, we cannot conclude that any of them have any permanent value in reversing the fundamental disorder. They alleviate the symptoms and behaviour, teach strategies that help people to understand others and accommodate them better, and reduce serious behaviours such as self-harm, but underneath very little has changed. This does not mean that the personality will stay exactly the same, as there are changes with age and circumstances, but our valiant attempts to change it by our special treatments only chip away at the edges.

Once we accept this, we have a refreshing set of approaches that will lessen the impact and importance of personality disorder while being aware it may still be lurking in the background. One of these is nidotherapy, discussed in the next chapter. Another is to use our personality problems positively. We have just carried out a very large study[4] of a psychological treatment for people who worry excessively about their health, commonly called health anxiety. The treatment was very effective, and five years after treatment finished those who had the treatment were much better than those who did not have it. We assessed personality status at the beginning of the study and were surprised to find that those who had mild personality disorder (mainly in the negative affective domain) showed the greatest benefit of all, and had a much better outcome than those with no personality disturbance). When we looked into this more closely we found that this personality group had been much more consistent in attending their treatment sessions and completed the course much better than others.

So here we have clear evidence of the benefit of personality disorder. It is fair to add that most other studies suggest that personality disorder is a hindrance to success,[5] but this may be because nobody has thought of using the personality disturbance positively before. I have certainly been aware of this in

my own practice for years. Sometimes the best treatment combination for a medical condition is a complicated one involving
several drugs or other forms of therapy, taken at precise times
during the day. When my patient is a highly conscientious
person, often extending into the personality disorder range, I
am confident that the treatment regime will be followed exactly
as prescribed.

If you, or someone else you know well, has mild or moderate
personality disorder the strategies for dealing with it can involve
the same approach as for personality difficulty, but with rather
more effort. The main form of management is nidotherapy (see
Chapter 9). The other, somewhat neglected, way of managing
the problem is to use your personality strengths to compensate
for the negative effects of the disorder.

This is the first time that the words 'personality strengths'
have been used in this book. This may seem odd. The trouble is
that in all the learned expositions on personality disorder there
is virtually nothing on personality strengths. I have also been
guilty of not taking this into account in my own work on personality disorder. In the first chapter of this book I described my
own personality in terms of its difficulties. I did not dwell on
personality strengths as they were not relevant to my attempted
illustration that personality both changes and stays the same,
in different ways, during the course of life. But without a description of my personality strengths nobody can really make
an overall judgement of my personality.

Personality strengths are present even in those with significant personality disorder. I am sure you will be able to remember
occasions when a person whom you know well rose to an occasion and behaved in a much more positive and affirmative
way than they would have done normally. These are often big
occasions like giving a speech at a wedding, arguing with a celebrity at a public meeting, impressing people at a job interview
or coping with the loss of a loved one. It seems people are able

to draw on reserves of strength at times of adversity and stress. So why are they not able to do this routinely? The simple answer is that they can't. The habits of personality disorder too often inhibit the enterprise that is in us all. Let us take one example from my own experience.

> Maureen was excessively shy and could not tolerate social situations or large groups of people. She was always extremely anxious in these situations and so did everything possible to avoid them. This anxiety had affected her work, where she generally underperformed as an office worker and was felt to be a bit of a wimp by her superiors.
>
> But she was not a wimp, and she had her wits about her. She noticed at work that some of her senior colleagues never seemed to be around even though they were supposed to be working full time in the office. Four of them appeared to be involved in covering for each other when they were not around. As a consequence, other more junior staff such as Maureen had to do greater amounts of work and were blamed if they faltered in these tasks and made the occasional mistake. Maureen had mentioned it to her immediate supervisor, who merely told her not to be a troublemaker and to get on with her own work.
>
> Despite Maureen's fear of large social occasions she felt the only way forward was to go to the top. Strictly speaking, it was not her preferred idea at all. It was just that her father, a former trade union representative, had convinced her that this was the only way forward. So at the company's Christmas party, where all the senior management sat at the top table, Maureen had her opportunity.
>
> She went straight to where the managing director was sitting.
>
> 'Excuse me, sir,' she said, blushing, but this was not going to stop her. 'I do not want to spoil the occasion but I have something very important to say to you. It will only take about two minutes.'
>
> 'Yes, my dear. But this is not a time and place to discuss such matters – come and see me in my office during working hours.'
>
> 'But I am not allowed to leave my office during working hours and would have no chance of seeing you then. I promise you it will take a very short time and it is in your interest to listen to me [her father had stressed this line to her in advance].'
>
> In the end she was persuasive enough to get him to leave the table, retire to a corner of the room, and tell him about the shenanigans in the office.
>
> She was not at all sure that he had taken this in and returned to

her seat at the back of the hall in some confusion, not least because by this point everyone was looking at her, which increased her social anxiety. But it worked. An internal investigation was carried out and three of the four conspirators were dismissed. Maureen was looked upon in a new light and shortly afterwards achieved promotion. When others said how astounded they were at the way she had been so brave in conquering her anxiety, she replied, 'You may not realize, but I feel like this most of the time, so an extra notch up on my fears does not make much difference.'

There are other ways of using your personality strengths. Those that are strong and positive can be used to reduce stress in your life[6] so that you choose where you will be most comfortable. Other people can also use their personality strengths to deal with others who have personality disorder. One of the other books in the Sheldon series, *How to Love a Difficult Man*,[7] illustrates this well. By adapting yourself to fit in with the foibles and difficulties of others you reinforce yourself. You can draw a parallel with haemophilia and the regular injections of the clotting agent. When in personality difficulty, give yourself an injection of personality strengths.

When it comes to the other end of the personality spectrum – severe personality disorder – I am much less confident. The proportion who seek treatment is relatively low and, as you might expect, most of them are in the borderline category. They may respond to one of the psychological treatments described in the previous chapter but they may also break off and go their own way.

For many others, especially those who show their personality abnormality in the form of aggression, it is very difficult to find any form of treatment that has long-lasting benefit. This is partly because so many in this group refuse to engage in any form of treatment. The only light at the end of the tunnel is the increasing evidence that with advancing age these personality features get less, and many have lost their most difficult personality problems by the age of 55.

My patient Melanie, whom I rashly said would improve by the age of 50, is now a little better and no longer creating chaos in the centre of London. But I think the main change has just been the passage of time, not the many attempts to intervene over the years. 'You'll never be able to change me, Peter,' she once proudly said, 'I am incorrigible.'

What does concern me over the current management of those with severe personality disorder is the excessive use of coercion. This is perceived simply as punishment, and whatever else psychology has taught us about personality disorder in the last 50 years, the main conclusion is that reward works and punishment fails. This is the area we need to be working on.

9

Nidotherapy

One of the fundamental reasons why personality disorder is perceived as such an unpleasant diagnosis is the notion of untreatability. But it is not untreatable, and I have been trying to get this message over to my colleagues for more than 50 years. The mistake is to equate personality with disorder. Our underlying personalities do persist and it is fair to regard them as 'ingrained', but when the first diagnostic descriptions of personality disorder were formulated, 'ingrained' wrongly became attached to personality disorder, and has persisted ever since.

All the evidence shows that personality disorder is an unstable diagnosis. Over time it changes more than any other mental condition. Why? The answer is simple, it depends on circumstances. This is where the treatment called nidotherapy comes into view. Nidotherapy is the systematic and collaborative manipulation of the environment to improve mental health, and it is admirably suited to personality disorder. It is named after the Latin word for nest, *nidus*, a very good example of a natural accommodating environment.[1] Nidotherapy involves a therapist working out what environmental changes would best help someone, and then working with the person to make them happen. But of course this formal therapy, if it really deserves such a title, is only one very small part of environmental change.

We make changes in our environments – and this includes social and personal environments, not just physical ones – all the time. We do not like the kind of job we are doing, even though we thought it might be ideal at first, and so we leave and get another one. We enter into relationships that also seem to be ideal but then go badly wrong. So we break them off. If we have any form of personality difficulty we probably come across these situations more often than others. The idea behind nidotherapy is that we do not allow these things to happen willy-nilly, but organize our lives, on our own or with help from others, so that they do not happen and our lives run more smoothly.

We have already heard that the only form of personality disorder that has an established set of treatments is the borderline one. But by far the biggest proportion of those who have personality difficulties are those who are not borderline. Why are there so few treatments for these people?

The main reason for this disparity is that those who have the extremely unpleasant symptoms of emotional dysregulation are desperately keen to get rid of them. So they consult doctors and other therapists repeatedly, often falling out with them and making many impulsive changes of doctors, even though this does not turn out to be too helpful. Most other people with personality problems do not seek treatment; we can call them treatment-resisting. This is not as odd as it sounds. People want to hold on to their personalities. They do not want them distorted in such a way so that they no longer recognize what they feel or who they are. They may consult a doctor with symptoms that are related to their personality problems but they are not asking for their personalities to be altered in any way.

Nidotherapy comes in many different forms

The advantage of nidotherapy is that it does not ask people to change their personalities but to adapt them in such a way that they fit in better with the environment. Here are a few examples from people I have treated, all shortened to emphasize the main components.

> Philip did not like being promoted. He liked working in his laboratory where everything was predictable and he was in control. In the laboratory he did not have to talk to anybody if he did not want to,

and most of the time he certainly did not want to talk to people, as he found most people annoying. He lived on his own and was more than happy in his own company. But because he had been so successful in his laboratory work he had been promoted to be head of department. This involved supervising a lot of people he did not like and did not understand. They annoyed him and he annoyed them, and this led to many complaints about his management style. After brief nidotherapy the problem was solved by his return to the laboratory.

Mildred was married with three children. She lived in a poor neighbourhood and had always lacked confidence since being bullied at school. Unfortunately, the people who bullied her were still living locally and she was often made fun of and ridiculed when she went shopping or was involved in social events. She was perpetually anxious and expected problems around every corner. After nidotherapy assessment it was felt that her home environment was an important cause of her continuing problems and, with the family's full approval, an application was made for her to move to a completely different area a few miles away. This transformed her, and in a completely new setting she felt free to be herself for the first time in her life.

Nigel was a troublesome adolescent. He was always getting into trouble at school and had been excluded on more than one occasion. He also told elaborate lies that led to major problems at home and at school. After several appointments in nidotherapy it became clear that his aggressive behaviour was directly related to expectations about his future career. He had been pressured to succeed in academic subjects but these were clearly not appropriate for him. After meetings at school he was transferred to a programme that led to an apprenticeship scheme where he performed very well. All his aggressive behaviour then disappeared.

Ethel was a woman of 56 who had been diagnosed with personality disorder and recurrent depression since her early twenties. Between the ages of 23 and 50 she had been continuously in psychiatric care and had received a host of treatments, both drug and psychological, including specific interventions for borderline personality disorder, and also electro-convulsive therapy, for her many symptoms. These had very little effect. She had also made several suicide attempts by overdose and had to be admitted to hospital, sometimes finishing up in intensive care.

Five years ago her psychiatrist had occasion to visit the family home after Ethel's latest relapse and overdose. He had been trained in nidotherapy and quickly realized that the relationships at home were highly abnormal. After further evaluation with Ethel they agreed that the 'nidotherapy solution' was for Ethel to leave home, as she was dominated and belittled there by her parents and they made unnecessary demands on her to look after them. When this was presented as a therapeutic answer to her parents they accepted this and Ethel moved out to stay independently. She remained on good terms with her parents and was much better mentally. At the time of writing, over five years after the introduction of nidotherapy, she is very well and free of symptoms, both of personality disorder and depression.

These examples illustrate perfectly that personality disorder is a fluctuating condition. Philip had a mild personality disorder, with the detached domain dominating, and while he was working in the laboratory nobody noticed any problems. It was only when he was promoted to a position of management that the difficulties associated with his personality structure came out, but they were immediately reversed again when he returned to the laboratory. Yes, his personality was ingrained, but his disorder was so short lived it hardly deserves the title.

Mildred had been to her GP many times with anxiety symptoms but the underlying cause of these, her low self-esteem, lack of confidence and fear of others, was part of a personality disorder dominated by anxiousness. Even after the move to a different area she remained anxious, but all the reinforcing elements that made it worse in the old environment were absent. So she was able to reform her life in a way that nobody had thought possible before.

Nigel illustrates why personality problems, particularly when associated with aggression and antagonism, should be dealt with early in life rather than leaving them to the adult years. In his case it is all too easy to see how continued aggression could lead to generalized delinquent behaviour and criminal offences in later life. By intervening early this was prevented.

Ethel's case, which you can read in full elsewhere,[2] illustrates why you should never give up hope if you have a long-term mental disorder. Although her apparently complete recovery is unusual, it does emphasize the fundamental importance of the environment in all its forms – relationships with others, feelings of personal worth and satisfaction, and the physical environment – in influencing mental illness.

Nidotherapy is not yet an established treatment in mental health, and it may never become one in the formal sense. But it is expanding its influence and is being used in many other countries, including Sweden, Australia, Canada and Iran, as it is straightforward, cheap to administer, and its principles are easy to understand (see <www.nidotherapy.com>). It offers hope to many people with personality problems who recognize that things are not exactly right in their personality structures but do not want to consult health professionals.

Its principles have been described fully elsewhere,[3] but there is much opportunity to try it out for yourselves. If, after reading this book, or suspecting that you have personality difficulties already, you want to make a start on sorting it out, you could do worse than carry out one of the central components of nidotherapy, a full environmental analysis, in which you analyse every part of your physical, social and personal environment to see if the personality problems you identify can be minimized or removed by making an appropriate change.

Other people can help in this task too. What is now called social prescribing involves listening to advice from others, whether or not they are health professionals, about activities you could take up, new people you could meet, and how you could spend your spare time. These may appear trivial or obvious, but sometimes the obvious is not seen by someone in the middle of personality difficulties, even though it may be crystal clear to someone else.

When we consider all the various forms of treatment that can be given for personality disorder, environment must be at the forefront. We are currently involved in a large research study in which we followed people with common mental illnesses and personality problems for more than 30 years. Over the course of this long period this group has had a tremendous number of interventions for mental illness. But when asked what intervention has helped them most, environmental change is coming very near the top. So wherever you are on the personality spectrum, and whatever gloom you may feel about recovery, do not forget that environmental change could be the solution just round the corner.

10

Drug treatment

There are a number of myths about psychiatrists that often appear in the popular press. These are reinforced by journalists who should be more interested in truth than good copy.

1 They have little idea what they are doing or why, as their practice is not based on science.
2 They are very friendly with pharmaceutical companies and by prescribing lots of drugs they get kickbacks.
3 They go into the profession because they have failed to get into a more prestigious speciality.
4 When their drug treatments fail, they just prescribe more drugs as they have nothing else to offer.

I am not going to rebut these, but in describing the drug treatment of personality disorder some of these myths can be explained.

The reasons why most people with personality problems do not seek treatment has already been explained. It is only those who have the borderline condition who ask repeatedly for treatment, as their symptoms are so devastatingly awful they cannot wait to have them relieved. It may seem odd at first that the many who do not want their problems treated are denying themselves the opportunity of benefit. But, when you think about it, many of the problems we now regard as difficulties in personality were not always so. For the cave dweller in Neolithic times it was useful to have people around you who were abnormally aggressive and violent, who were dependent and timorous and clung on to their children, and who were exceptionally fussy and well organized. Today's odd personalities had evolutionary benefit and they are not going to disappear suddenly from Homo sapiens.

But there is absolutely no benefit from the emotional dysregulation of borderline personality, and this should be clear from earlier chapters. No matter when it occurred in society over the millennia of human existence it would have caused similar problems. When symptoms are highly unpleasant there is an understandable demand for immediate relief. Sometimes the need for relief is shown in curious ways, such as cutting your skin, pulling out your toenails or taking overdoses. Other people, including doctors, often have great difficulty in understanding how these behaviours can lead to relief, but they do.

So it is not surprising that many consultations in general practice, accident and emergency department of hospitals, and psychiatric centres are urgent and emotionally laden events. Psychological treatments have great value but they cannot be given as emergencies unless there is a pre-specified plan that allows emergency contact to be part of a treatment programme. More often than not, this does not exist, and under these circumstances it is very difficult not to reach for the prescription pad in deciding what to do.

But what drugs are available, and do they help? The most frequently prescribed drugs are tranquillizing ones such as diazepam (Valium) and others from the same group (benzodiazepines), but other sedative drugs such as the major tranquillizers, like olanzapine (used in larger doses for the treatment of major mental illness such as schizophrenia), are almost equally used. Other drugs prescribed are the so-called mood stabilizers used for the treatment of bipolar disorder (lithium, sodium valproate, lamotrigine) and a range of different antidepressants such as fluoxetine, mirtazapine and paroxetine.

In a recent survey of 2,600 people with emotionally unstable personality disorder attending mental health services, 92 per cent were taking at least one of these drugs, with 16 per cent taking four or more.[1] So you would expect that they might be of some value. But they are not, or at least not after a day or so of treatment. Many of these drugs are sedative, and this effect is more or less immediate, so the terrible anxiety and tortured feelings that accompany emotional dysregulation are quelled to some extent. But it does not last.

When we get into this situation we are in danger of getting on a roller-coaster of what is called polypharmacy, the taking of many different drugs after no single drug appears to be effective. It is easy to guess what happens next. Drug A seems to have some effect in the first day or so after it is taken. For reasons that are not completely clear, this benefit does not last. Another appointment is requested, often as an emergency again. 'I think it's helping, Doctor, but it's also wearing off. Can I have something else to give it a boost?' So the doctor, trying to be helpful but having no indication of recommended treatment here, gives drug B to reinforce the effects of drug A.

Before too long the person can be taking three or four drugs simultaneously. We now get a rerun of the poem by Goethe, 'The Sorcerer's Apprentice'. In this story the young understudy of a sorcerer gets tired of fetching water with a broom and invokes some of his master's magic by trying to get the broom to do the job for him. But the young man has an incomplete knowledge of magic, and very soon afterwards the broom takes over and increases its speed. The young man panics, breaks the broom into pieces, but each piece forms itself into a complete broom and brushes even faster, so everything gets completely out of control. Then the master sorcerer returns and normality is restored. The pharmaceutical sorcerer's apprentice behaves in the same way. Every drug seems to add to the symptoms, needing another drug to assist, and then another drug to counteract the effects of the first or accentuate the effects of the second, till eventually the poor person is taking tablets four times a day but essentially staying in the same place as far as relief of the original problem is concerned.

We still do not know whether drug therapy has any real advantage in the treatment of personality disorder independently of other mental illness. There is a well-known adage in medicine – absence of evidence is not evidence of absence – and it may be that the important studies that show that drug treatment is effective have not yet been carried out. But until these revelations come, we should treat all drug therapy for personality disorder with a certain degree of scepticism and only regard its use as a crisis measure.

If you read about the treatment of personality disorder there is usually quite a bit to say about drug treatment. Many people, some in positions of considerable authority, maintain that drug treatment has particular value in the treatment of personality disorder, even though it is not considered to be the main treatment. I used to feel the same, even though I had some scepticism, but when I chaired a representative group of experts in psychiatry, psychology, pharmacy and statistics, and service-users with experience, our group came to a different conclusion. These meetings took place over two years and looked at all the evidence of treatment value from every possible source. This was a guideline development group of the National Institute for Health and Care Excellence (NICE), and our recommendations were expressed succinctly: 'Drug treatment should not be used specifically for borderline personality disorder or for the individual symptoms or behaviour associated with the disorder.'[2] There is nothing more to be said until further evidence is available.

11

Outcome

Your personality stays the same throughout your life. This is only half true. Your basic personality structure does stay more or less the same, but it can be knocked off course by child abuse, neglect, illness and severe stress. Sometimes these changes persist, especially after the severe trauma of war or if they occur early in life when personality is developing.

For the average person, tiptoeing through life with the occasional hiccup and intermittent joys, personality persists in its basic structure. When we approach old age there are natural changes in lifestyle that have an impact on personality. We do less, our horizons become smaller, relationships usually become fewer. In our own research we have found that, on the one hand, obsessional symptoms, especially rigidity and detachment, become more pronounced than they were earlier in life. On the other hand, aggression and impulsive behaviour become less marked. Are these changes real personality ones or are they just a natural accompaniment to getting old? I suspect they are a mixture of both. The average 75-year-old ex-boxer does not relish getting into fist fights, but does not like his daily routine to be changed repeatedly. The sociable whist-drive organizer and charity fundraiser suffers a steady loss of fellow extroverts as she gets into her eighties, downsizes to a cheerless flat and steadily loses her social skills. She is now regarded as a cranky old woman who suffers fools poorly and is increasingly isolated.

The basic personality may still be identifiable, but it only comes through in glimpses, and it is seen as different by others. When Dylan Thomas wrote about his ageing father dying peacefully without fighting back against the depredations of senility, he was expressing a young man's frustration with the passivity and acceptance of an old man gradually slipping into oblivion. 'Why don't you fight in the way you used to, Dad; what has changed?' Age has changed everything, and part of the old personality has probably withered too.

We need to know a lot more about change in personality before we can provide remedies. In the new classification of personality disorder there is a condition called 'late-onset personality disorder' that arises later in life. This can come about in different ways. A man who has always been somewhat difficult and irritable but has seldom been involved in conflict because his tolerant and understanding wife has accommodated and covered up his whims is left alone and rudderless when his wife suddenly dies. All his underlying personality difficulties are now exposed and friends and relatives see an irascible, confrontational and unpleasant man whom they claim never to have encountered before. But they have, if only in a minor form, because until this time his aberrations have been compensated.

Personality and illness

Illness may also alter personality. When people develop dementia it is not only brain power that diminishes but personality changes also. This is not surprising, as the seat of personality is also in the brain, but it alters in very many ways. Some people become excessively aggressive and irritable – it is not surprising that training in coping with violence is mandatory for care workers – whereas others appear to retreat into apathy and disinterest with none of their former personality features on show. Yet others seem to return to the personalities of their childhood as though they were retreating in time and cheating the clock. But the behaviours of dementia are complex and should not commonly be attributed to personality. As mentioned earlier, the recognition of environmental factors and their reversal by nidotherapy may change difficult behaviours into pleasant ones, so it is a mistake to assume that trouble will persist no matter what you do.

Chronic illness, in any form, is also a jolt to personality. An active sportsman cut down by motor neurone disease, a knitwear enthusiast with swollen fingers handicapped by rheumatoid arthritis, a lifelong birdwatcher who goes blind – all have to make big adjustments to their lives. This is when personality strengths such as determination and persistence can come into play and make a virtue out of disability. You only have to see the success of the Invictus Games for war veterans to realize the virtues of new horizons never previously seen.

For reasons based on hope and guesswork rather than evidence, all classifications of personality disorder conclude there is less manifestation of disordered behaviour with advancing age. You can tell from the above account that this is not exactly correct. There are dozens of ways in which personality can change, some positive and some not, but they are not entirely unpredictable. Personality is not a wild animal that goes its own way – it keeps its essentials but can be guided and kept under control.

We cannot forget the jesters in the pack, borderline disorder and psychopathy. Do these change too over time? There are many who would dearly like to know the answer, but, as usual, the jester plays tricks again. The good news is that many of the features of the disorder do disappear over time. Mary Zanarini, working at McLean Hospital and the University of Harvard in the USA, has carried out a long-term follow-up: after 16 years, 9 out of 10 people previously diagnosed could no longer be diagnosed as personality disordered. The bad news is that fewer of them had recovered and more had experienced relapses than with other personality disorders.[1] This mixture of hope and despair is difficult to come to terms with. I only hope we will be able to explain why before too long.

I come back to the beginning of this book. I am now in my

seventies and am comfortable with my personality difficulty. I still blurt out when I should be quiet, I still get annoyed by petty authority and my life is still overshadowed unduly by the work ethic. But these are under control and I know how to lessen them. I hope that most of you also are feeling the same way or, if not, can see ways forward to achieving this goal. Using our personality strengths and accepting that at least some of the difficulties we may have with other people are generated by us alone are the keys to understanding. The title of this book can then be changed. There is no longer a 'beast within'; it is just a pussycat.

Notes and further reading

Preface

1 Lewis, G. and Appleby, L. (1988) 'Personality disorder: The patients psychiatrists dislike', *British Journal of Psychiatry*, July, 153(1):44–9. This article gives a view on personality disorder from the psychiatrist's angle – one that has not changed much over the 30 years since its publication.

1 What is personality?

1 Salinger, J. D. (1951, 2010) *Catcher in the Rye*. New York: Little, Brown and Company; London: Penguin. Worth reading again and again. Shows how adolescent angst can look like personality disorder.

2 Normal and abnormal personality

1 Reprinted from World Health Organization (1992) *International Classification of Diseases* (10th revision – ICD-10). Geneva: WHO. Pp. 222–3. Copyright 1992. This will be superseded by ICD-11 in 2018.
2 Schneider, K. (1923) *Psychopathic Personalities* (original German text trans. M. W. Hamilton, 1958). London: Cassell. Of historical interest.
3 Hare, R. D. (1991) *The Hare Psychopathy Checklist* (revised edition). Toronto: Multi-health Systems. Not to be looked at in detail unless you are a serious researcher.
4 Ronson, J. (2011) *The Psychopath Test*. London: Picador. An amusing read, but please do not take it too seriously. This is a journalist pretending to be like Voltaire's *Candide*, going into the big wide world of psychopathic personality and being *so* surprised.
5 Harris, T. (1991) *The Silence of the Lambs*. New York: St Martin's. Thomas Harris looked at all the very worst aspects of psychopathy and remodelled them in the form of Hannibal Lecter.

3 The difference between mental illness and personality disorder

1 Tyrer, P., et al. (2001) 'Instrumental psychosis: The syndrome of the Good Soldier Švejk', *Journal of the Royal Society of Medicine*, 94:22–5. Worth thinking about.
2 Newton-Howes, G., Mulder, R. and Tyrer, P. (2015) 'Diagnostic neglect: The potential impact of losing a separate axis for personality disorder', *British Journal of Psychiatry*, 206(5):355–6. A cry to retain the separation of personality disorder from mental illness – unsuccessful.
3 Newton-Howes, G., et al. (2014) 'Influence of personality on the out-

come of treatment in depression: Systematic review and meta-analysis', *Journal of Personality Disorders*, 28(4):577–93. Big paper showing that personality difficulties impair recovery from depression.

4 Tyrer, P. (1978) 'Drug treatment of psychiatric patients in general practice', *British Medical Journal*, 21008–10. A descriptive paper only.

5 Tyrer, P., et al. (1983) 'Gradual withdrawal of diazepam after long-term therapy', *Lancet*, 321:1402–6. First evidence that personality factors are major influences on withdrawal symptoms from benzodiazepine tranquillizers.

6 Montagu, L. (2017) 'Desperate for a fix: My story of pharmaceutical misadventure' in James Davies (ed.), *The Sedated Society: The causes and harms of our psychiatric drug epidemic*. London: Palgrave Macmillan. A view from the patient's side of the benzodiazepine withdrawal problem.

7 Kim, Y.-R., et al. (2016) 'Schedule for personality assessment from notes and documents (SPAN-DOC): Preliminary validation, links to the ICD-11 classification of personality disorder, and use in eating disorders', *Personality and Mental Health*, 10(2):106–17. A scale to assess personality difficulties from records and notes, not interviews.

8 Self, W. (2013) 'Psychiatrists: The drug pushers', *The Guardian*, 3 August. A rant about psychiatrists being the cause of drug misuse – even though these drugs are predominantly prescribed by GPs. Like Jon Ronson, he writes in arresting prose, but this should not be confused with veracity.

9 Burns, T. (2014) *Our Necessary Shadow: The nature and meaning of psychiatry*. London: Penguin. An honest account of what it is like to be a jobbing psychiatrist and some of its tribulations.

10 Tyrer, P., et al. (2017) 'Cognitive behaviour therapy for health anxiety in medical patients (CHAMP): Randomised controlled trial with outcomes to five years', *Health Technology Assessment*, 21(50):1–58. This is a heavy 54-page document, but it can be downloaded free from NIHR Library and will encourage those people with personality disorder who feel they always draw the short straw. Here they come out tops!

11 Tyrer, P. (2015) 'Personality dysfunction is the cause of recurrent non-cognitive mental disorder: A testable hypothesis', *Personality and Mental Health*, 9:1–7. This is a hypothesis that needs to be tested, but early evidence suggests it may be right.

4 Politics and personality

1 Kim, Y.-R., et al. (2016) 'Schedule for personality assessment from notes and documents (SPAN-DOC): Preliminary validation, links to the ICD-11 classification of personality disorder, and use in eating disorders', *Personality and Mental Health*, 10(2):106–17.

2 Frances, A. (2016) *Huffington Post* blog, 9 June.

3 Owen, D. (2012) *The Hubris Syndrome: Bush, Blair and the intoxication of power*. London: Methuen. David Owen's magisterial discussion about hubris, from someone who knows it well, as a government minister, party leader and peer of the realm.

4 Tyrer, P. (2016) *The Death of King John*. Newark: Blue Frog Publications. A play based on the last days of King John's life, when he started to realize he had a personality disorder and was universally disliked.

5 When is personality disorder formed?

1 Kagan, J. (1997) *Galen's Prophecy: Temperament in human nature*. Boulder, CO: Westview Press. Covers the range of Kagan's work, beginning with the philosopher Galen, who in AD 192 first linked personality to the main four body humours – black bile (melancholic), yellow bile (choleric), blood (sanguine) and phlegm (phlegmatic). Not a bad classification for 1,850 years ago.

2 Livesley, J., et al. (1993) 'Genetic and environmental contributions to dimensions of personality disorder', *American Journal of Psychiatry*, 150:1826–31. A scholarly paper showing that environmental and genetic factors mix together roughly equally, thus making it wrong to concentrate on one rather than another or to make simple statements such as 'there is a gene for aggression'.

3 Frick, P. J., Ray, J. V., Thornton, L. C. and Kahn, R. E. (2014) 'Can callous-unemotional traits enhance the understanding, diagnosis, and treatment of serious conduct problems in children and adolescents? A comprehensive review', *Psychological Bulletin*, 140(1):1–57. A thoughtful review of the concept of callous and unemotional traits in children and their possible persistence.

4 Bowlby, J. (1969) *Attachment and Loss*, New York: Basic Books, and *Separation: Anxiety and Anger*, London: Hogarth Press, 1973. Worth reading to illustrate how much information it is possible to deduce from close observation of young children.

5 Fonagy, P., Lutyen, P. and Strathearn, I. (2011) 'Borderline personality disorder, mentalisation and the neurobiology of attachment', *Infant Mental Health Journal*, 32:47–59. One of many publications drawing together attachment theory, its relevance to adult personality disorder and its likely biology.

6 The new classification

1 Tyrer, P., et al. (2015) 'Classification, assessment, prevalence and effect of personality disorder', *Lancet* 385:717–26.

2 Dahl, R. (1984, 2013) *Boy: Tales of Childhood*. London: Jonathan Cape and Penguin Books. P. 164. © The Roald Dahl Story Company Limited.

7 Borderline personality disorder

1 Linehan, M. M. (2015) *DBT Skills Training Manual* (2nd edition), New York: Guilford Press. Very many books have been published on the psychological treatments for borderline disorder, both tomes for trainers and self-help for novices. This is a heavy book, but it includes what most

authorities feel is the most effective component of dialectical behaviour therapy, skills training. This book covers the skills of emotional regulation, mindfulness, interpersonal effectiveness and distress tolerance. Many of these elements are very similar to those in other therapies, but go under different names.

2 McFarlane, J. (2017) 'And they call it a f****** science!', *British Journal of Psychiatry*, 210(4):300. A poem in a psychiatric journal reminding the psychiatrist what it feels like to be described as borderline.

3 Tyrer, P., et al. (2003) 'Treatment-rejecting and treatment-seeking personality disorders: Type R and Type S', *Journal of Personality Disorders*, 17(3):265–70. Article showing how many people do not want treatment for their personality difficulties.

4 Bateman, A. W. and Krawitz, R. (2013) *Borderline Personality Disorder: An evidence-based guide for generalist mental health professionals.* Oxford: Oxford University Press. A good account of structured clinical management for borderline personality disorder that includes most of the elements of the specific therapies.

5 Taylor, B. (2015) *The Last Asylum: A memoir of madness in our times.* Chicago, IL: University of Chicago Press. A book to read if you feel that there is no possible way of getting your personality difficulties solved. Barbara Taylor charts her own passage across the very stormy seas of personality disorder with only one navigator, her psychoanalyst, staying by her side throughout. She gets to a safe haven in the end.

8 Taming personality disorder

1 Tyrer, P., et al. (2003) 'Treatment-rejecting and treatment-seeking personality disorders: Type R and Type S', *Journal of Personality Disorders*, 17(3):265–70.

2 Akiskal, H. (1985) 'Borderline: An adjective in search of a noun', *Journal of Clinical Psychiatry*, 46(2):41–8. The title may be sufficient to explain what this is all about.

3 Yang, M., et al. (2010) 'A national survey of personality pathology recorded by severity', *British Journal of Psychiatry*, 197(3):193–9. An article predating the new classification that shows personality difficulties as well as disorders are surprisingly common.

4 Tyrer, P., et al. (2017) 'Cognitive behaviour therapy for health anxiety in medical patients (CHAMP): Randomised controlled trial with outcomes to five years', *Health Technology Assessment*, 21:50.

5 Newton-Howes, G., et al. (2014) 'Influence of personality on the outcome of treatment in depression: Systematic review and meta-analysis', *Journal of Personality Disorders*, 28(4):577–93.

6 P. Tyrer, *Overcoming Stress* (2nd edition). London: Sheldon Press. The account of personality in this book shows how stress can be reduced by suiting your personality to circumstances.

7 Good, N. (1987) *How to Love a Difficult Man.* London: Sheldon Press.

Men have just as many personality difficulties as women, but have a tendency not to consult professionals and talk about it as much. This book shows how women can deal with their dearly beloved, but deeply frustrating, men.

9 Nidotherapy

1 Tyrer, P. (2009) *Nidotherapy: Harmonising the environment with the patient*, London: RCPsych Publications. The principles of nidotherapy, given in much more detail than it is possible to go into here. (Second edition, 2018.)
2 Spears, B., et al. (2017) 'Nidotherapy in the successful management of comorbid depressive and personality disorder', *Personality and Mental Health*, 11:344–50. The full account of an extraordinary recovery from personality disorder with nidotherapy.
3 Tyrer, P., 'Principles of nidotherapy in the treatment of persistent mental and personality disorders', *Psychotherapy and Psychosomatics*, 72:350–6. An account of the core principles of nidotherapy (see also <www.nido-therapy.com>).

10 Drug treatment

1 Paton, C., et al. (2015) 'The use of psychotropic medication in patients with emotionally unstable personality disorder under the care of UK mental health services', *Journal of Clinical Psychiatry* 76(4):e512–18.
2 National Institute of Health and Clinical Excellence (2009) 'Borderline personality disorder: Recognition and management' (CG78). London: Department of Health. This long document can be downloaded easily from the NICE website. It has quite a lot of jargon that is difficult to follow, but the executive summary is clear on how the disorder should be managed. The guidance was reviewed in 2015 and no changes were recommended.

11 Outcome

1 Zanarini, M. C., et al. (2012) 'Attainment and stability of sustained symptomatic remission and recovery among patients with borderline personality disorder and axis II comparison subjects: A 16-year prospective follow-up study', *American Journal of Psychiatry*, 169(5):476–83. Mary Zanarini has published a series of papers on a cohort of patients treated at a hospital near Harvard in Massachusetts (it is worthwhile emphasizing this as it may not be representative of treatment elsewhere) and these show that, although the symptoms (and consequent diagnosis) of borderline personality disorder tend to disappear rapidly over time, general functioning and life satisfaction does not improve nearly as much.

Index

Overcoming Common Problems Series

Seleted titles

A full list of titles is available from Sheldon Press,
36 Causton Street, London SW1P 4ST and on our website at
www.sheldonpress.co.uk

The Assertiveness Handbook
Mary Hartley

Breaking Free
Carolyn Ainscough and Kay Toon

Cataract: What You Need to Know
Mark Watts

Cider Vinegar
Margaret Hills

Coping Successfully with Irritable Bowel
Rosemary Nicol

Coping Successfully with Panic Attacks
Shirley Trickett

Coping Successfully with Ulcerative Colitis
Peter Cartwright

Coping with Anxiety and Depression
Shirley Trickett

Coping with Blushing
Professor Robert Edelmann

Coping with Bowel Cancer
Tom Smith

Coping with Brain Injury
Maggie Rich

Coping with Childhood Allergies
Jill Eckersley

Coping with Chronic Fatigue
Trudie Chalder

Coping with Dyspraxia
Jill Eckersley

Coping with Gout
Christine Craggs-Hamilton

Coping with Polycystic Ovary Syndrome
Christine Craggs-Hinton

Coping with Postnatal Depression
Sandra L. Wheatley

Coping with Thyroid Problems
Dr Joan Gomez

Curing Arthritis – The Drug-Free Way
Margaret Hills

Curing Arthritis Diet Book
Margaret Hills

Depressive Illness
Dr Tim Cantopher

Eating for a Healthy Heart
Robert Povey, Jacqui Morrell and Rachel Povey

Free Your Life from Fear
Jenny Hare

Help Your Child to Get Fit Not Fat
Jan Hurst and Sue Hubberstey

How to Accept Yourself
Dr Windy Dryden

How to Cope with Difficult People
Alan Houel and Christian Godefroy

How to Keep Cholesterol in Check
Dr Robert Povey

The Irritable Bowel Diet Book
Rosemary Nicol

Letting Go of Anxiety and Depression
Dr Windy Dryden

Living with Alzheimer's
Tom Smith

Living with Asperger Syndrome
Dr Joan Gomez

Living with Autism
Fiona Marshall

Living with Fibromyalgia
Christine Craggs-Hinton

Living with Food Intolerance
Alex Gazzola

Living with Rheumatoid Arthritis
Philippa Pigache

Living with Sjörgren's Syndrome
Sue Dyson

Losing a Baby
Sarah Ewing

Losing a Child
Linda Hurcombe

Overcoming Jealousy
Dr Windy Dryden

Understanding Obsessions and Compulsions
Dr Frank Tallis